Philip R. Stone

111 Dark Places in England That You Shouldn't Miss

T0150545

emons:

For my Rachael Dorrian and our 'Paddington Bear' adventures.

© Emons Verlag GmbH
All rights reserved
© Photographs by Philip R. Stone, except see p. 236–238
© Cover icon: shutterstock.com/koya979; russ witherington
Layout: Eva Kraskes, based on a design
by Lübbeke | Naumann | Thoben
Maps: altancicek.design, www.altancicek.de
Basic cartographical information from Openstreetmap,
© OpenStreetMap-Mitwirkende, OdbL
Editing: Karen E. Seiger
Printing and binding: Grafisches Centrum Cuno, Calbe
Printed in Germany 2021
ISBN 978-3-7408-0900-3
First edition

Did you enjoy this guidebook? Would you like to see more?
Join us in uncovering new places around the world on:
www.111places.com

Foreword

I have been writing about people visiting the dead for a long time. I first turned to the 'dark side' when a student of mine introduced me to 'dark tourism'. That is, the act of traveling to sites of death, disaster, or the seemingly macabre. The idea of tourists visiting places that portray heritage that hurts is filled with many dilemmas. Of course, people have long been drawn to sites of death and fatality. In ancient times, gladiatorial games were a leisure mainstay of the Roman Empire. During the medieval period, public executions of criminals were spectator events. And, in 19th century Europe, morgue tours to encounter corpses were a common travel itinerary.

As a social scientist, I am fascinated as to why particular deaths are remembered, by whom, and how our dead are (re)presented within the visitor economy. Sadly, the world is littered with sites of tragedy. Our mistakes and misfortunes are exposed by landscapes of adversity, accidents, and calamity. Visiting and remembering our dead is a cultural phenomenon – we attach importance to certain kinds of death and the dead. In turn, the dead can become significant to the living and warn us of our mortality. Yet, commemoration is challenged by politics of remembrance, commercialism, and conflict in memorialisation, as well as the ethics of interpretation. Dark tourism is further challenged by consumer behaviour and visitor experiences.

I wrote this book to provide an authoritative yet accessible guide into the dark places of England. Each of the 111 places in this book offers a provocative and emotive account of the site and its uniquely dark story. I wrote it for you to discover the sites, do additional research on its themes, and respect the difficult heritage of places of pain and shame. Ultimately, this inimitable guidebook permits you to sightsee in the mansions of the dead, while having deference to those deceased.

111 Dark Places

1 The Bampton Icicle Stone
Death by icicle

Bampton, a historic Charter Town, lies on the edge of the Exmoor National Park. Saxon in origin, the small town is full of character, with many conserved buildings dating to the time of William the Conqueror. The *Domesday Book* of 1084/85 provides Bampton's status by referring to it as the 'Hundred of Baentona'. The town, built around the wool and pony trade, and later quarrying, was granted a Royal Charter in 1258 by King Henry III. The Bampton Fair, held on the last Thursday of October, celebrates local foods and livestock, as well as crafts and traditional skills of Exmoor. It is one of the oldest surviving Charter Fairs in England.

Bampton was also a site of battle in the English Civil War. In 1645, the town was burned and looted, and only a few buildings remain pre-dating that event. As Royalist and Parliamentary forces in the Civil War clashed, the Royalists marched from nearby Tiverton Castle and spent four days torching the town. The Devon Clubmen, who were headquartered in Bampton, were a group of landowners armed with clubs, cudgels, and pitchforks. They attempted, with little success, to defend their property.

Bampton is also home to a little known occurrence that sparks curiosity. In the early 12th century, St Michael and All Angels Church was built on the site of previous places of Celtic worship. Yew trees planted around 1483 still stand proudly in the graveyard, and the church is home to town stocks last used as punishment in 1862. However, at the base of the church's tower on the west side is a stone tablet (a 1950s replacement) commemorating the death of an 18th century local lad. The odd rhyming inscription reads: *IN MEMORY OF THE CLERK'S SON / "Bless my i.i.i.i.i.i. / Here he lies / In a sad Pickle / Killed by Icicle" / IN THE YEAR 1776*

This unfortunate victim remains unknown, along with his name, age, his family, and how he actually died.

Address St Michael and All Angels Church, Station Road, Bampton, Tiverton, EX16 9NG, +44 (0)139 833 2885, www.hukeleymissioncommunity.org/locations/st-michael-all-angels-bampton | Getting there Train to Tiverton Parkway, then a 15-minute taxi ride | Hours Unrestricted | Tip Berry Pomeroy Castle is a romantic ruin with a history of ghostly intrigue (Berry Pomeroy, Totnes, Devon, www.english-heritage.org.uk).

2 Charlotte Dymond Memorial

Murder and miscarriage of justice

On 14 April, 1844, 18-year old Charlotte Dymond was brutally murdered. Her body was found several days later at Rough Tor on the desolate Bodmin Moor. Her throat had been cut. At first, the tragic killing appeared to be a result of spurned love, but controversy about the murder and its verdict has become local folklore.

Charlotte Dymond was a domestic servant at Penhale Farm on the edge of Bodmin Moor. During her employment, she began a romantic relationship with Matthew Weekes, a young, disabled and illiterate farm labourer. They set off together for a Sunday walk onto the lonely moors, but Charlotte never returned home. Weekes fled to Plymouth but was soon arrested and charged with Charlotte's murder. He pleaded not guilty.

Weekes was tried at Bodmin Assizes, where a jury returned a guilty verdict in only 35 minutes, based on circumstantial evidence, a poor defence and unreliable witnesses. Sentenced to death, Weekes was hanged at Bodmin Gaol on 12 August, 1844 and buried in the prison's coal yard. In the intervening years, there has been much doubt as to Weekes' guilt, particularly as another lover – Thomas Prout – was implicated in the murder after the trial.

Charlotte Dymond's murder became a tabloid sensation and the stuff of Penny Dreadful fiction. Death-obsessed Victorians appeared to be entranced by the killing of a young girl at the hands of a lover during a secret moorland rendezvous. An estimated 20,000 spectators watched Weekes' execution, and *The West Briton* newspaper reported that a fete with donkey rides and refreshment stalls was held at Rough Tor, with 10,000 attendees. People paid a penny to see the spot where the murder took place. A granite obelisk was erected in 1845 to commemorate Charlotte Dymond.

Address Roughtor Road, Bodmin Moor, Cornwall, PL32 9QG | Getting there By car, take A 39, exit at A 395 and follow the turns to Rough Tor Car Park. The memorial is situated on moorland near a stream. | Hours Unrestricted | Tip A stone headstone in 2017 replaced the wooden cross marking Charlotte's grave. You can visit her actual burial site at St David's Church (Davidstow, near Camelford, PL32 9XT).

3 Exercise Tiger Memorial
The forgotten dead of friendly and enemy fire

'Exercise Tiger' was the codename of a training operation to prepare troops for D-Day and the liberation of Nazi-occupied Europe (see ch. 70). Supreme Commander of Allied Forces Dwight D. Eisenhower wanted drills for the invasion to be as realistic as possible, including the use of live ammunition. Slapton Sands in Devon was chosen as the exercise location because the beach closely resembled Utah Beach, a site of the Normandy landings. Over 3,000 local residents were told to leave six weeks before the exercise with no explanation. Then, on 27 April, 1944, as Exercise Tiger commenced, live artillery shells slaughtered over 400 American soldiers due to a timing blunder. Kept secret by authorities for decades and still not formally recognised by the US Government, the calamity was the worst case of friendly fire during World War II.

The shocking event became a double tragedy on 28 April, 1944, when nine German E-boats passing through Lyme Bay stumbled upon the exercises. They opened fire on the mock-invasion, killing 639 men. The harrowing scenes of corpses washing up onto the beach would be replicated on D-Day six weeks later at Normandy.

With over 1,000 soldiers slain, the irony is that Eisenhower achieved realism in his dress rehearsal attack. Survivors received no leave to recover from the trauma of Exercise Tiger. They were sworn to secrecy, under threat of court martial, and a media blackout followed so as not to compromise the impending landings of D-Day.

In 1984, the late Ken Small raised a sunken Sherman tank from local waters – a remnant of that fateful day in 1944. After much bureaucracy, Small 'purchased' the tank from the US government for $50. He pursued the idea of a memorial to end 50 years of silence. The Sherman tank, with a plaque to commemorate Small's endeavours, now rests on a cobbled plinth and honours the sacrifices of those who died.

Address Exercise Tiger Memorial, Torcross, Devon, TQ7 2TQ,
www.exercisetigermemorial.co.uk | Getting there By car, take A 379 to Torquay | Hours
Unrestricted | Tip Lynmouth Flood Memorial Hall is where a devastating flood in 1952
created conspiracy theories about secret RAF cloud-seeding experiments (Lynmouth
Street, Lynmouth, Devon, www.visitlyntonandlynmouth.com).

4 Kitty Jay's Grave

Denied a Christian burial because of 'self-murder'

At a crossroads of a country lane in the Dartmoor National Park is a burial mound and gravestone. Supposedly the final resting place of Kitty (Mary) Jay, an 18th-century orphan, the grave has become folklore. While tales of Jay have been romanticised and embellished over the years, including stories of the supernatural, her grave is a black spot on burial rites of yesteryear.

Jay was abandoned as a baby and left at the Poor House in Newton Abbot in the late 1700s. She was given the surname 'J' (stylized as Jay) by the orphanage, but because 'Jay' was a slang term for a prostitute, she was given the Christian name Mary. Jay grew up to become a teenage apprentice at Canna Farm in the parish of Manaton, where she became known as Kitty. While at the farm, she was either raped by a farm labourer or fell in love with the farmer's son. Consequently, Jay became pregnant and was dismissed from service. Penniless and in disgrace – and in fear of being ostracized – the young Kitty Jay committed suicide by hanging herself in the farm's barn. At the time, suicides were judged guilty of 'self-murder' and punishable by withholding consecrated burial sacraments. Spirits of suicide victims were feared by the living. A way of dealing with this fear was to bury corpses at a crossroads (often with a stake through the heart), so any wandering ghost would be disoriented as to which way to haunt.

Crossroad burials for suicides have been documented as early as 1510, with its origins in Anglo-Saxon times. They were abolished by law in 1823, after the suicide of Lord Castlereagh, the Foreign Secretary, who helped defeat Napoleon. However, the memory of Kitty Jay, a downtrodden orphan girl, has lasted longer than the people who denied her a Christian burial. Today, her grave is always adorned by votive offerings of flowers, pennies and mementos by passing visitors and secular-pilgrims.

Address Manaton, Newton Abbot, Devon, TQ13 9XF | Getting there The grave is located one mile north-west of Hound Tor at the Green Lane to Natsworthy. | Hours Unrestricted | Tip Instead of numerals, the 'My Dear Mother' church clock at St Peter's Church spells out a memorial to a lost loved one (Buckland-in-the-Moor, Newton Abbot).

5 Museum of Witchcraft & Magic

A bewitching cauldron of curiosities

The Museum of Witchcraft and Magic is a Cornish cabinet of curiosities, where witches, piskies and spriggans are displayed. Reimagined tales of folklore and magic are told at this independent museum in the picturesque fishing village of Boscastle. With significant collections of paraphernalia relating to witchcraft, the museum is both a pilgrimage site for modern witches as well as an authority on the occult. Exhibits include a reconstruction of an 18th-century 'cunning woman' cottage, complete with various herbal remedies and divination tools. The museum also contains exhibits devoted to witch trials, the Pagan religion of Wicca, as well as other esoteric practices such as ceremonial magic, alchemy, Satanism and Freemasonry.

The museum was originally founded by folk magician Cecil Williamson in 1951 and located on the Isle of Man. Assisted by prominent Wiccan and resident witch Gerald Gardner, the pair fell out, and Williamson brought his collection to England. Located first at Windsor and then at Bourton-on-the-Water before moving to Boscastle in 1960, the museum faced violent opposition, including the hanging of dead cats outside the premises. In 1996, Graham King took over the museum and removed many of the sensationalist objects. King also organised the burial of Joan Wytte, who had died at Bodmin Jail in 1813, having been accused of witchcraft. Her corpse had been at the museum for many years and was laid to rest in local woodlands.

In the past, witches were persecuted for felony acts rather than for blasphemy. Whilst the museum works to build narratives that illustrate witchcraft over time, it positions magic and witchcraft as a significant contemporary force. The museum offers a focus for occult heritage, but ongoing problems of romanticised Pagan myth-making ensure the collections remain a cauldron of controversy.

Address The Harbour, Boscastle, Cornwall, PL35 0HD, +44 (0)184 025 0111, www.museumofwitchcraftandmagic.co.uk | Getting there By car, take B 3263 or B 3266 to Boscastle, continue on B 3263 to Drs Hill, and New Road to the destination on the left | Hours See website for seasonal hours and tickets | Tip Visit Merlin's Cave in the coastal cliffs beneath Tintagel Castle, once home to the wizard of Arthurian legend (South-West Coastal Path, Castle Road, Tintagel, Cornwall).

6 __ William Donaghy Memorial
The tragic case of a dead school teacher

Dartmoor has inspired enigmatic myths and legends, including the haunting of pixies, a headless horseman, and a mysterious pack of spectral hounds. During the Great Thunderstorm of 1638, the village of Widecombe-in-the-Moor was said to have been visited by the Devil himself. However, the tragic demise of William Donaghy is one shadowy event that is remembered by a difficult-to-find boulder memorial deep inside the moor heartlands.

On 21 February, 1914, two farmers discovered the fresh corpse of a young man near Hartland Tor. There was no evidence of foul play or self-harm, but he was wearing inadequate attire for the winter moor weather. The man was wearing a blue spotted tie and a Swiss watch, and his possessions included a Dartmoor guide book, £20 in gold coins (£2,400 at today's rates) and a cloakroom ticket dated 4 February from Exeter Railway Station. When police redeemed the ticket, they recovered a bag that had been deposited under the name 'Jones'. It contained a revolver and ammunition, a knife, a watch and chain and a mourning ring inscribed *1817*.

The body was identified as 33-year-old, Liverpool-based William Donaghy, a science teacher, who worked at Warrington Technical School and who had been diagnosed with 'morbid melancholy'. On 21 November, 2013, Donaghy left his brother a note that read, 'I am going away. Please settle my affairs.' He was never seen alive again.

What did Donaghy do after he left Liverpool? What was he doing on the moor so far from home? And why did he have weapons under an assumed name? After his funeral in Liverpool, the boulder near where his body was found was engraved – there is no record of who inscribed it. In 1934, another Warrington teacher was found dead close to where Donaghy died, and yet another died at Beachy Head in Sussex. Both were wearing blue spotted ties and Swiss watches.

Address Dartmoor National Park, Devon, +44 (0)162 683 2093, www.legendarydartmoor.co.uk/donaghy-mystery-the.htm, hq@dartmoor.gov.uk | **Getting there** Car parking at Postbridge National Park Visitor Centre, PL20 6TH. Follow the right-hand side bank of East Dart River for about two miles northwards. Pass Hartland Tor before arriving. The boulder is set in some gorse at 364 metres. | **Hours** Unrestricted | **Tip** Trek to Hollowcombe Bottom, the site of a mysterious Dartmoor Pony Massacre in 1977 (Near Postbridge, Devon, www.legendarydartmoor.co.uk/ufo_ponies.htm).

7 Bevin Boys Memorial
Forgotten World War II heroes sent to the mines

Over 48,000 men were conscripted into an underground army that many have forgotten. Between 1943 and 1945, ten per cent of male military conscripts between 18 and 25 years old were randomly picked and forced into coal mining. By 1943, mining had lost 36,000 workers, as many men opted to join the armed forces. Faced with a labour shortage, the minister of Labour and National Service, Ernest Bevin, proposed compulsory mining conscription. Conscripts became known as 'Bevin Boys,' though many feared the social stigma of not being in uniform, and many resented being coerced into mining. Bevin Boys also faced resentment down the mines from experienced miners because of the quantity of coal dug and subsequent payments.

Life as a miner was dangerous, and accidents were commonplace. Over 5000 men were killed in British mines during World War II. The first Bevin Boy to be killed accidentally was Henry Hale from London, aged 18, who died only a month after his training in 1944. Bevin Boys disabled by accidents did not get a pension, and for those killed, their dependents did not receive benefits. Yet the conscription did not stop until 1948, when most servicemen had already been demobilized. But, unlike military personnel, Bevin Boys did not have the right to return to their original jobs. In 1950, all records of Bevin Boys were destroyed, and former miners could not prove their wartime service.

This lack of recognition has been a stain on England's war memorialisation. It was not until 2004 that Bevin Boys were allowed to march past the cenotaph on Remembrance Sunday – whilst other civilian groups had long been represented. Fortunately, in 2007, the British Government stated mining conscripts would receive long-overdue recognition. In 2013, the Bevin Boys memorial at the National Memorial Arboretum (see ch. 19) was unveiled, in remembrance of the young men who served underground.

Address National Memorial Arboretum, Croxall Road, Alrewas, Staffordshire, DE13 7AR, +44 (0)128 324 5100, www.thenma.org.uk, info@thenma.org.uk | Getting there Train to Lichfield Trent Valley, then a 15-minute taxi ride | Hours Daily 10am–5pm | Tip The Staffordshire Regiment Museum shares its military history from 1705 to the present-day (DMS, Whittington, Lichfield, www.staffordshireregimentmuseum.com).

8_ The Coffin Works

Conserving funerary heritage

In the heart of Birmingham's old Jewellery Quarter is a small factory whose industry relied on death. The Coffin Works is the former factory of the brothers Alfred and Edwin Newman, who produced some of the finest funerary furniture when it opened in 1882. Originally brass founders, the factory's commercial mainstay became funerary furniture. However, after emphasizing being the best coffin furniture factory in the UK, the company ceased trading in 1998, due to a reluctance to modernise and the fact that metal components were banned in cremations. The factory opened as a museum in 2014, a time capsule of social and industrial history.

With its working machinery and funerary products, such as coffin handles, urns and ornaments, linings and shrouds, the factory is left as it was in the 1960s, preserving the Victorian engineering. The Newman brothers produced coffins for the funerals of Winston Churchill, Joseph Chamberlain, the Queen Mother, and Princess Diana. Coffin Works is not only testament to funerary heritage, but it also highlights a UK death disposal industry that is worth about £1 billion annually, with over 600,000 funerals taking place every year, an estimated 4,000 funeral directors, and the average funeral cost of a funeral at £4,184 (in 2021).

Coffin Works is also home to an extensive and unique collection of funerary artefacts that contribute to understanding changing attitudes towards death and, indeed, life over the past century. In 1935, the first major initiative to replace the term 'undertaker' with 'funeral director' emerged. It was this effort to professionalise the status of the trade that propelled the Newman brothers' business. Those operating in the funeral industry wanted social recognition for their care of the dead. As a result, the 'sights, sounds and smells' of Coffin Works as a funerary furniture factory encapsulates this care, even when death rites are ever changing.

Address T13-15 Fleet Street, Birmingham, B3 1JP, +44 (0)121 233 4790,
www.coffinworks.org, newmanbrothers@coffinworks.org | Getting there Train to
New Street or Snow Hill | Hours Fri–Sun 10.45am–4pm; reservations required | Tip
Warstone Lane Cemetery Catacombs, also known as Brookfields or Mint Cemetery,
hosts a tiered semicircle of tombs. It's also a former place of 'unhealthy vapours'
(Icknield Street Hockley, Birmingham).

9 Eyam Plague Village
Dammed by a pestilential death

Nestled within the picturesque Peak District National Park is the historic village of Eyam (pronounced 'EEM'). Inhabited since Anglo-Saxon times, the village became famous due to its unique response to the bubonic plague in 1665-66. The Plague had ripped through England during various pandemics in the Middle Ages, peaking with the Black Death of 1346-1353. The Oriental rat flea was the primary vector for transmitting the deadly *Yersinia pestis* bacterium, which caused an agonising death with an 80% mortality rate.

When the Plague reached Eyam, the whole village, under the leadership of Reverend Stanley and Reverend Mompesson, decided to quarantine itself rather than flee the Plague. No one was allowed to enter or exit the village during the fourteen months the disease took hold. The Plague apparently arrived at the village on fleas within a bundle of cloth from London ordered by local tailor George Vicars. He became the first victim, along with 260 other villagers (out of 800). Families were required to bury their own dead in unconsecrated ground. But the quarantine prevented the disease from spreading into surrounding areas.

Just outside Eyam is a small graveyard, known as the Riley Graves. Here, Elizabeth Hancock buried her husband and six of her seven children over a period of eight days in August 1666. Marked rocks around the village indicated the *Cordon Sanitaire*, or boundary of the doomed community. Villagers left money disinfected with vinegar in return for foodstuffs brought by outsider merchants.

Eyam reported the last case of Plague in England, and the self-isolation of the village became a medical case study for treating infectious diseases. In 2020-21, the global COVID-19 contagion also saw whole communities self-isolate. Eyam Museum in the village is where to begin to explore this plague of the past and learn lessons for modern pandemics.

PLAGUE COTTAGE

Mary Hadfield, formerly Cooper, lived here with her two sons, Edward and Jonathan, her new husband, Alexander Hadfield and an employed hand George Viccars

George Viccars, the first plague victim, died on 7th September 1665
Edward Cooper, aged 4 died on the 22nd September 1665
Jonathan Cooper, aged 12, died on the 2nd October 1665
Alexander Hadfield d...
3rd ...

Address Eyam Museum, Hawkhill Road, Eyam, Derbyshire, S32 5QP, +44 (0)143 363 1371, www.eyam-museum.org.uk, contact@eyam-museum.org.uk | **Getting there** Train to Grindleford, transfer to bus 257 Bakewell to Coach Park | **Hours** See website for hours and tickets | **Tip** Visit the grave where 'Little John', the most famous of Robin Hood's legendary 'Merry Men', is reportedly buried at St Michael's Centre (2 Main Road, Hathersage, Derbyshire, S32 1BB).

10__The Ilkeston Giant

A dead showman mighty in stature

Stanton Road Cemetery is a Victorian burial ground in Ilkeston, established by lifelong non-conformist Matthew Hobson, a miller and a grocer. Rather than burying his wife Hannah at nearby St Mary's churchyard in 1862, he placed her in the grounds of what was then Field House, without authority. A year later, Hobson established the Ilkeston General Cemetery Corporation. With social class accompanying the 19th century dead (see ch. 84), graves could be purchased in three categories: First, Second and Third class. The 'first class' dead were buried on higher ground with grand tombstones marking their demise. 'Third class' plots were at the back of the cemetery, where up to nine corpses would occupy a single grave. Eventually, the grave would be emptied and the process started again.

A local celebrity of the cemetery is Samuel Taylor, known as the Ilkeston Giant. Born on 4 June, 1817 in Little Hallam, Taylor was unusually tall for a man of that period. By adulthood, he was 7 feet and 4.5 inches tall. Struggling to find employment because of prejudice, Taylor visited a travelling fair at Castle Donnington in 1832. He remarked, 'I entered the exhibition… and discovered a man, perhaps about six feet three. All eyes were turned upon me. I stood beside the giant and made him look very insignificant' (from *The Witch, the Weird, and the Wonderful* 2015 blog).

An altercation between the two tall men ensued, and Taylor won the fight. The fair owner appointed Taylor as the new giant. Taylor would marry the owner's daughter. After various jobs, including running a pub, Mr and Mrs Taylor created their own travelling fair. However, on 3 June, 1875, after fracturing his thigh, Taylor died at the age of 59. A life-sized, wood sculpture at Stanton Road Cemetery, carved by Andrew Frost, marks Taylor's grave and commemorates a showman mighty in stature.

Address Stanton Road Cemetery, Stanton Road, Ilkeston, Derbyshire, DE7 5FW | **Getting there** Train to Ilkeston | **Hours** Unrestricted | **Tip** 'Tip the Faithful Sheepdog' was a heroic pup who never left her dead master's side. Look for a memorial to this good girl at Derwent Dam Viewpoint (Hope Valley, off Snake Road (A57), Peak District).

11 *Jigger*, the Miner
Shiny colossus homage to tragically killed miners

Coal as a primary fossil fuel powered huge economic and socio-cultural developments of the Industrial Revolution in the 18th and 19th centuries. Yet the human cost to extract this black rock from depths of the earth is significant. Over the past three hundred years, there have been tens of thousands of colliery accidents and miner deaths around the world.

One such death memorialised in the form of a giant sculpture is that of Jack 'Jigger' Taylor. Jack was a miner tragically killed in a colliery disaster in the Brownhills location of the West Midlands. The area is famed for its mining heritage, including the 'Black Country' – once renowned for its smoky ironwork foundries and forges and its rich shallow coal seams.

The father of three, Jack was known as a happy-go-lucky man and remembered throughout the community for his love of whistling and singing. He started work underground in 1929 aged just 14 and was nicknamed 'Jigger' from an early role operating machinery that drilled into the coalface. Jack died when the roof collapsed at Walsall Wood colliery in 1951.

In 2008, Jack's great-grandson Jak Groves (then aged 13) won a local competition to name the £700,000 artwork memorial by artist John McKenna. Today, a 40-foot-tall, five-tonne, stainless steel statue pays homage to the dead miner and all those who have lost their lives in the coal mining industry. The shiny colossus stands proud in the centre of a traffic roundabout, overlooking a landscape once pockmarked by heavy industry. At the mining industry's peak, up to 80 per cent of Brownhills' population worked in the sector, including children as young as 11 years old in the 19th century.

Today, mining as an industry is all but gone. *Jigger* serves both as a celebration of the business that first built the town, as well as a commemoration of all those who have perished digging for coal.

Address High Street & Chester Road, Brownhills, West Midlands, WS8 6EB | **Getting there** Train to Shenstone, then a 10-minute taxi ride. Look for *Jigger* on a roundabout at this busy traffic junction. | **Hours** Unrestricted | **Tip** Discover more industrial heritage at the Black Country Living Museum (Tipton Road, Dudley, www.bclm.co.uk).

12 Knife Angel
'Save a Life, Surrender your Knife'

The *Knife Angel* is an emotive, 27-foot-high sculpture that captures social consciousness. Housed at the British Ironwork Centre, the *Knife Angel* is fabricated from over 100,000 knives surrendered in police amnesties, as well as knives used in crimes and killings. The artwork is made of flick and pen knives, machetes, samurai swords, and kitchen knives, and it has become a memorial to those killed or affected by knife crime in the UK.

The idea for the sculpture was conceived by Clive Knowles, chairman and founder of the British Ironwork Centre in coordination with artist Alfie Bradley. They wanted social change, education and community collaborations to be the *Knife Angel's* legacy. Refused funding by the British government for fear the artwork would show the country in a bad light, the project was nevertheless supported by all 43 UK police constabularies. The statue was unveiled in 2018.

Also known as the *National Monument Against Violence and Aggression*, the *Knife Angel* raises awareness and understanding of how violent behaviour affects communities. With blades blunted and forming the Angel's wings, some knives are inscribed with messages from victims' families, as well as felons who express remorse for their actions. The sculpture is powerful in both size and meaning, and Bradley poses the Angel's eerie face to express a sense of despondency. Looking down in sheer despair, the jagged angel seems to be asking, 'Why would you do this? What have you done?'

Sharing a message of anti-violence, the *Knife Angel* often tours the UK accompanied by workshops and other educational activities. Knife crime in the UK is a national embarrassment and a scourge of society, particularly for teenagers. With complex underlying social and cultural causes, knife crime creates traumascapes of killings and violence. The *Knife Angel* brings messages of hope and peace.

Address Aston Way, Morda, Oswestry, Shropshire, SY11 4JH, +44 (0)800 688 8386, www.britishironworkcentre.co.uk, info@britishironworkcentre.co.uk | **Getting there** Train to Gobowen, then a 10-minute cab ride | **Hours** Wed–Sun 10am–4pm | **Tip** At the Timber Jacks Club, you can safely immerse yourself in 'axe throwing' – a lumberjack sport (Flexspace, Unit 49, Shrewsbury, www.timberjacks.club).

13 The Last Sin-Eater

Pawning your soul to the Devil

In the tranquility of St Margaret's churchyard in the village of Rat-linghope is a plinth monument for Richard Munslow. Born in 1833, Munslow is thought to be the last 'sin-eater' of England when he died in 1906.

Sin-eaters were paid to consume a meal over a corpse in order to 'eat' the sins of the deceased. The food was believed to absorb the sins of the unconfessed dead, thus absolving the soul of the deceased. Consequently, sin-eaters 'carried' the sins of the dead whilst living and often suffered a 'social death,' having become community outcasts, despite their valued services. Sin-eaters were also thought to prevent the sin-ridden dead from becoming ghosts and allowed an untroubled passage into Heaven.

Sin-eating was a macabre ritual that appears to derive from Welsh culture, as it was practiced in the Welsh Marches and the shires that border England. As an ancient custom, sin-eating may have its origins in the early Israelites' practice of transferring sins to a 'scapegoat'. Similarly, in Meso-American civilisations, Tlazolteotl, the Aztec goddess of vice, would cleanse the soul by 'eating its filth'. In Christianity, Jesus Christ has been interpreted as a universal archetype for sin-eaters, offering His life to atone for human sins. Symbolic relics of sin-eating today include eating funeral biscuits, or burial cakes, which are still produced in some parts of the world.

Sin-eaters were typically vagrants who essentially pawned their souls to the Devil. However, Richard Munslow was a farmer of some substance. A clue as to why he became a sin-eater might lie in the fact that three of his children died young. The north face of the plinth is inscribed, 'Suffer little children to come unto me, and forbid them not, for such is the Kingdom of Heaven.' Munslow's monument was restored in 2010 after featuring on BBC Radio 4's 'History of the World in 1,000 Objects'.

Address St Margaret's Churchyard, Ratlinghope, Shrewsbury, Shropshire, SY5 0SR, +44 (0)158 865 0580 | Getting there Train to Church Stretton, then a 25-minute taxi ride | Hours Unrestricted during daylight hours | Tip Visit the graves of the 'Nine Men of Madeley' – victims buried together who plunged to their death in a mining lift tragedy in 1864 at St Michael's Church (Church Street, Madeley, TF7 5BN, www.ninemen.org).

14 National Civil War Centre

A lasting legacy of civil conflict

The English Civil Wars (1642–1651) took place in the British Isles between King Charles I (and his successor, Charles II) and opposing groups in each of the kingdoms, including Parliamentarians in England, Covenanters in Scotland and Confederates in Ireland. The Civil Wars began in 1642 in England. Charles I raised an army against the wishes of Parliament, ostensibly to deal with Irish insurrection.

The conflict was about governance, power and religious (in)tolerance. This legacy is retold at the National Civil War Centre, dedicated to the 17th-century Civil Wars. It features diverse exhibits and living history events. Visitors can immerse themselves in a time when neighbour fought against neighbour, and when political unrest brought bloodshed across the nation.

Led by pious Oliver Cromwell, the first war was won by Parliamentary forces ('Roundheads') at the 1645 Battle of Naseby. The second war saw Cromwell and his New Model Army defeat the Royalists ('Cavaliers') at the Battle of Preston in 1649. Cromwell also massacred the Irish Confederates, snuffing out any Royalist cause. Convicted of treason, King Charles I was beheaded and the monarchy abolished.

Exiled Charles II formed an army of English and Scottish Royalists, which prompted Cromwell to invade Scotland in 1650. In 1651, Cromwell won at the Battle of Worcester and ended the 'wars of the three kingdoms'. Once declaring, 'Keep your faith in God, but keep your [gun] powder dry,' Cromwell – as Lord Protector – ruled the British Isles from 1653 until his death in 1658. His son, Richard, succeeded as Lord Protector, but he lacked ability, and the Protectorate ended in 1659. In 1690, Parliament and the monarchy under King Charles II ushered in The Restoration. Cromwell was exhumed from his grave in 1661 and symbolically executed and beheaded. His head was left on a spike at Westminster Hall until 1685.

Address National Civil War Centre, 14 Appleton Gate, Newark, Nottinghamshire, NG24 1JY, +44 (0)163 665 5765, www.nationalcivilwarcentre.com | Getting there Train to Newark Northgate or Newark Castle | Hours Wed–Sat 10am–3pm | Tip The Queen's Sconce in Sconce and Devon Park is a fascinating preserved remnant of the English Civil War (Boundary Road, Newark, Nottinghamshire, www.newark-sherwooddc.gov.uk/sconceanddevon).

15 National Cyclists War Memorial

Homage to those who cycled for King and country

The village of Meriden has long claimed to be the geographical heart of England. Standing proud on Meriden's village green is an unusual war memorial. At 30 feet high, a Cornish granite obelisk commemorates all cyclists who died during World War I.

Cycling during the Edwardian period became symbolic of personal mobility. While bicycles had existed for decades, advancements made them faster, safer and cheaper. A cycling craze ensued with clubs established to foster a sporting and leisure activity. With the 1914 declaration of war, the British Army created the Army Cycle Corps. Originally, it was thought the corps could replace the outdated horseback cavalry, as bikes were quick, quieter and did not require feeding. During the conflict, though, thousands of army cyclists acted as reconnaissance scouts, often behind enemy lines, or as messengers trundling through shelled towns and trenches.

Exposed without armour or protection, and often riding at night under enemy fire, many soldier cyclists were killed in action. The first to be killed in World War I was Private John Parr, a cyclist infantry scout with the 4th Middlesex Regiment. On 21 August, 1914, he died in action at only 17 years old, having enlisted underage. Walter McGregor Robinson, known as the 'cycling journalist', reported the horror of trench warfare as he cycled across the Western Front.

Unveiled by Lord Birkenhead on 21 May, 1921, the National Cyclist Memorial inauguration was attended by over 20,000 people. In 1963, a bronze plaque was added to remember cyclists killed in World War II, including bicycled paratroopers during the second wave of D-Day in 1944. A remembrance service is held at the memorial every May, when cyclists from around the UK ride to pay homage to those who cycled and died for King and country.

16 National Holocaust Centre
A place of testimony to man's inhumanity

The Holocaust, also known as the Shoah, was the genocide of European Jews during World War II. Nazi Germany and its collaborators systematically murdered an estimated six million Jews, around two-thirds of Europe's Jewish population. Industrialised state murder enacted Nazi fascist doctrine, where mass killings were carried out in pogroms and shootings under a policy of annihilation through slavery in concentration camps and in gas chambers at extermination camps, including Auschwitz-Birkenau, Bełżec, Chelmno, Sobibór and Treblinka in occupied Poland. The Holocaust haunts contemporary imagination for the scale of atrocities committed by a genocidal state and its slaughter of entire groups determined by heredity. Roma gypsies, Slavs, communists, the disabled, Jehovah's Witnesses and homosexuals were also targets of persecution and gradual attrition.

Established in 1995 by two Methodist brothers, James and Stephen Smith, after their visit to Yad Vashem in Israel, the National Holocaust Centre remains the only UK museum dedicated to Holocaust remembrance. Set on the edge of Sherwood Forest and with a landscaped Memorial Garden designed for reflection and contemplation, the Centre is a vibrant memorial, a space for testimony and evidence, and a place of witness for all.

The Children's Memorial, dedicated to 1.5 million children killed during the Holocaust, is being built slowly by visitors to the Centre. Visitors are invited to select a stone and place it on the memorial, in tribute to the murdered youngsters. Exhibits include The Journey, a story which follows a fictional young boy living in 1938 Berlin. Holocaust survivors and oral history also feature prominently at the Centre. The Forever Project is an ambitious 3D interactive scheme designed to preserve the voices of Holocaust survivors for generations to come 'lest we forget'.

Address Acre Edge Road, Laxton, Newark, Nottinghamshire, NG22 0PA,
+44 (0)162 383 6627, www.holocaust.org.uk, office@holocaust.org.uk | Getting there Train
to Newark Northgate | Hours See website for hours and bookings | Tip Take a stroll along
Linby Docks, a quaint stone-lined stream that was targeted by the Nazis in World War II
after a blunder from Nazi propaganda broadcaster 'Lord Haw-Haw' (Main Street, Linby,
Nottinghamshire, www.linby.org.uk/heritage/linby-docks-restoration.php).

17 National Justice Museum

Bringing penal heritage to life

Penal heritage is brought to life at the National Justice Museum through immersive visitor experiences, courtroom re-enactments and over 40,000 crime and punishment artefacts. Intended to inspire people to become active citizens, the award-winning attraction reopened in 2017, having previously been known as the Galleries of Justice.

The museum is located within Nottingham's old Shire Hall and Gaol (jail). A court has existed at the site since 1375 and a prison from at least 1449. During medieval times, Sheriffs were appointed by the king, who kept the peace and collected taxes. The local, infamous Sheriff of Nottingham features heavily in Robin Hood folklore. Over the centuries, thousands of people have entered the building with an impending sense of dread. The entrance steps were the site of many public executions, with Thomas Gray the last person to be hanged in public in 1877. The jail closed in 1878, and the building became a police station in 1905. The Shire Hall continued to be a civil and criminal court until 1991.

Objects on display at the museum include the door of Oscar Wilde's prison cell from Reading Gaol, evidence from the 1963 Great Train Robbery and the prisoner dock from Bow Street Magistrates Court in London (now a boutique hotel). Other artefacts include the bathtub used in the 'brides in the bath' murders, for which George Smith was hanged in 1915. In the rear yard, visitors can climb a gallows used for executions. Prisoners executed on these gallows included Nazi radio propagandist William Joyce, otherwise known as Lord Haw-Haw. Though the death penalty was abolished in England in 1965, it remains a theoretical possibility for treason, piracy with violence and mutiny in the armed forces. The gallows, originally from Wandsworth Prison, were preserved in full working order and regularly tested as late as 1990.

Address High Pavement, Nottingham, NG1 1HN, +44 (0)115 952 0555,
www.nationaljusticemuseum.org.uk, info@nationaljusticemuseum.org.uk | Getting there
Train to Nottingham | Hours Fri–Mon 10am–5pm | Tip Look for the memorial plaque
of Frank Robinson, also known as 'Xylophone Man', who was a musically inept busker
who entertained with a child's metallophone (Lister Gate, Nottingham City Centre).

18_Polish Airmen Graves

Fearless foreigners fighting for Britain

After the fall of Poland in 1939, the Polish Air Force was evacuated to Romania and Hungary. Thousands of soldiers then found their way to France, where, in accordance with the 1921 Franco-Polish Military Alliance, Polish Air Force units were re-created. Polish pilots with obsolete planes fought valiantly against Nazi aggression, flying 714 sorties during the Battle of France. But when France capitulated in 1940, the Polish Air Force withdrew to the UK. Today, tranquil Newark Cemetery, one of numerous UK cemeteries for Polish airmen, holds 397 Polish war graves.

Initially, the RAF was unwilling to accept the independence and sovereignty of Polish forced soldiers, who had to wear British uniforms and were required to take two oaths – one to the Polish Government and one to King George VI. Despite their overwhelming experience and expertise, the Polish pilots were forced into basic training and given low ranks. However, after heavy RAF losses, the British relented in their snobbery, and the Poles were given their own squadrons.

Quickly achieving high 'kill rates' again, Polish pilots were often regarded as fearless, bordering on reckless. Flying Hawker Hurricanes, Polish squadrons claimed the largest number of enemy aircraft during the Battle of Britain. Nine of the squadron's pilots qualified as 'aces'. Sergeant Josef František was the top scorer with 17 planes, but he was later shot down and killed. Overall, 2,408 Polish airmen were killed during the war.

Many Polish sorties were flown from RAF bases near Newark. They used to fly over the cemetery upon return to acknowledge fallen comrades. A Polish Memorial Cross in Newark Cemetery marks the graves of President Raczkiewicz (head of wartime Polish government, d.1947) and General Sikorski (Commander-in-Chief and wartime Polish prime minister, d.1943), whose actual remains were returned to Poland in 1993.

Address Newark Cemetery, London Road, Newark-Upon-Trent, Notts, NG24 1SQ, www.newark.gov.uk/Cemetery.aspx | Getting there Train to Newark Castle or Newark Northgate | Hours Daily 7am–6pm | Tip In the Dukes Wood Nature Reserve, *The Oil Patch Warrior* is a memorial to US 'roughnecks', who secretly worked in the UK's only oil field in 1943 (Kirklington, Newark).

19 _ *Shot at Dawn* Monument

Soldiers executed by the State

The National Memorial Arboretum, situated on the edge of the National Forest, is the UK's centre of remembrance. With 350 provocative memorials in a 150-acre parkland, monuments, statues and cenotaphs are diverse and rich in symbolism. Together, they represent a broad population of society from military associations, charitable organisations and emergency services, to fraternity groups and individuals. New memorials are added to the Arboretum each year in a kind of *memorial mania*, demonstrating the inherent need to remember our significant dead.

However, one memorial stands out from the rest. Before post-traumatic stress disorder (PTSD) became medical parlance, World War I soldiers fighting in relentless battles and horrors of trench warfare suffered what was then called 'shell-shock'. Some absconded or could not fight any more and were hastily court-martialed for cowardice or desertion. The British military executed many of these young men and boys. The *Shot at Dawn* memorial is a poignant reminder of that injustice. Created by artist Andy DeComyn in 2000, the memorial commemorates 309 soldiers executed by the State. The *Armed Forces Act 2006* pardoned the soldiers posthumously, although the pardon did not affect any conviction or sentence.

The memorial portrays a young British soldier tied to a stake and blindfolded, ready to be shot by a firing squad. The statue is modelled on 17-year-old Private Herbert Burden, who lied about his age to enlist. He later suffered shell-shock and was executed for desertion. Surrounded by a semicircle of stakes, each of which are inscribed with names of other executed soldiers, *Shot at Dawn* is symbolic of the shameful shadows of our untreated armed forces. Yet, the Arboretum is also an uplifting place which honours the fallen, recognises service (see ch. 57) and sacrifice and, arguably, fosters pride in the country.

Address National Memorial Arboretum, Croxall Road, Alrewas, Staffordshire, DE13 7AR, +44 (0)128 324 5100, www.thenma.org.uk, info@thenma.org.uk | Getting there Train to Lichfield Trent Valley, then a 15-minute taxi ride | Hours Daily 10am–5pm | Tip Do not miss the Hanbury Crater, the largest non-nuclear explosion in history created when a bomb dump exploded in 1944 (Fauld Lane, Tutbury, Burton-on-Trent).

20_ Shrewsbury Prison

An excursion into a criminal's incarceration

Shrewsbury Prison offers excursions into a criminal's incarceration as you walk in the footsteps of former prisoners and prison guards. Penal heritage from Georgian times to the present day is retold through immersive visitor experiences and tours.

Influenced by the ideas of renowned prison reformer John Howard, the jail was constructed by Thomas Telford. The *1774 Gaol Act* called for jails to be improved from their medieval counterparts. Known as the 'The Dana', after Rev Edmund Dana, Shrewsbury Prison was completed in 1793 and rebuilt in 1877. For many years, the prison drew huge crowds to witness public executions, with posters sold as morbid souvenirs. The last public execution at Shrewsbury Prison on 11 April, 1863 saw 30-year-old Edward Cooper hanged for murder. Executed convicts were buried in unmarked graves within the prison grounds, where many still rest today. During redevelopment works in 1972, the remains of 10 unnamed hanged prisoners were exhumed and cremated. The prison is cited in the 1896 poetry series *A Shropshire Lad* by A.E. Housman, whereby the proximity of the prison to Shrewsbury railway station is noted: "They hang us now in Shrewsbury jail / The whistles blow forlorn / And trains all groan on the rail / To men that die at morn."

During the 1950s, executions at the prison were carried out by Albert Pierrepoint, the last hangman of Britain. Over a 25-year-career, Pierrepoint executed nearly 600 prisoners, including war criminals condemned at the Nuremberg Trials. The final execution at the prison was on 9 February, 1961 when 21-year-old George Riley was hanged for murder. The jail was decommissioned in 2013, and visitors today can see the old hanging room, explore the prison infrastructure and take 'CELLfies' in the prison cells. Visitors can also stay overnight and role-play a warden controlling prisoner machinations on 'A Wing'.

Address The Dana, Shrewsbury, Shropshire, SY1 2HR, +44 (0)174 334 3100, www.shrewsburyprison.com | Getting there Train to Shrewsbury | Hours Daily 10am–5pm | Tip Visit Lilleshall Monument to the 1st Duke of Sutherland (1758–1833), famed for his obscene wealth and controversial role in the Highland Clearances (9 Hillside E, Lilleshall, Shropshire).

21 — The Workhouse

Social savagery of dealing with paupers

Within a rural idyll close to the minister town of Southwell is an atmospheric Victorian workhouse. The Workhouse is an imposing National Trust building dating from 1824 that served as a place of last resort for the destitute. It was designed to house around 160 'inmates' – men, women and children – in workhouse uniforms, who were strictly segregated and made to work for subsistence. Workhouse jobs included picking oakum (stripping rope fibres for the caulking of ships) or crushing bones to make fertilizer.

The Workhouse is the best-preserved example of the 19th-century English workhouse system. Designed by William Adams Nicholson together with Rev John Becher, a social reformer and workhouse pioneer, the building remained a workhouse until 1929. Becher once remarked that 'an empty workhouse is a successful one.'

Victorians viewed poverty as a stain on the character of an individual and unemployment as idleness and an indulgence rather than any economic issue. The 'deserving poor' were sent to the workhouses as a deterrent to other paupers, and many workhouses profited greatly from their free labour. The *Poor Law Amendment Act 1834* aimed to stop welfare relief to the poor who refused to enter the workhouse. Over time, workhouses evolved from prison-like panopticons to places for the aged and infirm. *The 1948 National Assistance Act* completely eradicated the deterrent institution. The Workhouse provided temporary accommodation for the homeless until 1976 before being partially converted into an elderly residential home until the 1990s.

Strict discipline, poor diet and religious piety were hallmarks of the Victorian workhouse, and a 1905 Royal Commission helped abolish the deterrent institutions. Today, the Workhouse shines a harsh light on this cultural legacy and reminds us of social savagery of the cruel treatment meted out to the poor.

Address Upton Road, Southwell, Nottinghamshire, NG25 0PT, www.nationaltrust.org.uk/the-workhouse-southwell | Getting there Nearest rail station is Newark Castle (10 minutes by taxi); regular bus services from Newark, Nottingham and Mansfield stations | Hours See website for hours and reservations | Tip Visit The Sacacens Head, a 13th century inn, where the ill-fated King Charles I spent his last night of freedom (Market Place, Southwell, Nottinghamshire, www.saracensheadhotel.com).

22__ Clifford's Tower

A monument to York's turbulent and bloody past

Standing proud on its high mound, Cliffords Tower is all that remains of York Castle built by William the Conqueror in 1068. York has long been an important centre of political and ecclesiastical power in northern England. The Province of York is one of two provinces that make up the Church of England – the Archbishop of York is second only to the Archbishop of Canterbury. Settled by the Romans and known as *Eoforwic* ('wild boar settlement') in Saxon times, the city was renamed *Jorvik* by the Vikings in the 10th century.

Throughout York's turbulent history, the imposing tower has been both a fortress and jail, and it witnessed much bloodshed. The darkest episode for York's Jewish community occurred at the tower, where religious intolerance and greed resulted in violence and murder. On 16 March, 1190, anti-Semitic riots culminated in a massacre of 150 Jews. Stoked by Christian fundamentalism of Holy Land Crusades, the Jews took refuge in the tower. Local gentry, including Richard Malebisse and Philip de Fauconberg egged on a baying mob, as they saw the pogrom as a way to wipe out extensive debts owed to local Jewish money-lenders. The Jews barricaded themselves inside the tower, for fear of being murdered by an assembly of knights. Rather than renounce their Jewish faith, many chose to commit suicide, whilst others were killed when the mob set the tower on fire. After the massacre, the gentry burnt records of their debts, thus absolving repayments to the King.

As a jail and a debtor's prison, the tower housed some famous inmates. George Fox, founder of the Quakers, was held in 1665. The notorious highwayman Dick Turpin was also imprisoned here and executed in 1739 (see ch. 23). In 1890, the prison commissioners declared the tower a national monument. But it was not until 1978 that a memorial stone was laid at the tower's base to commemorate victims of the 1190 pogrom.

Address Clifford Tower, Tower Street, York, YO1 9SA, www.english-heritage.org.uk/visit/places/cliffords-tower-york | **Getting there** Train to York, then a 20-minute walk | **Hours** See website for hours and tickets | **Tip** At Baile Hill, you will see remnants of the oft-forgotten second castle that William the Conqueror built in York (Baile Hill Terrace, York, YO1 6DT).

23 Dick Turpin's Grave
A violent villain romanticised

Tucked away in a deserted graveyard opposite St George's Church in York is the proclaimed grave of England's most infamous highwayman, Richard (Dick) Turpin. Born in Essex in 1705 to John and Mary Turpin, Dick became a career criminal involved in poaching, burglary, murder and armed highway robbery. During the 18th century, travellers were often viciously attacked by 'highwaymen' – robbers on horseback.

Turpin was a violent man who joined the Essex Gang and terrorised the Home Counties. After most of the gang were captured by the authorities, Turpin, with his partner in crime Thomas Rowden, waylaid travellers and robbed them at gunpoint. While living in a cave in Epping Forest, Turpin was seen by Thomas Morris. Morris made a foolhardy attempt to capture Turpin, but the wanted outlaw shot and killed him. Under the alias John Palmer, Turpin fled to Yorkshire but was unable to keep out of trouble. In 1738, he was imprisoned at Beverley for shooting a man's cockerel and threatening to kill him. Turpin was then transferred to York Castle Gaol where his true identity was revealed.

Turpin was tried at York Assizes, condemned to death and paraded through York in an open cart on 7 April, 1739 to the gallows at Knavesmire (dubbed 'Tyburn' after the famous London execution site). Speaking calmly to his executioner, Turpin threw himself off the gallows and suffered slow strangulation by hanging. His corpse was taken to the Blue Boar Inn in Castlegate, where body-snatchers stole his body for dissection. His cadaver was apprehended and apparently reburied in lime at St George's Church.

In 1834, novelist William Ainsworth published *Rookwood*, with Dick Turpin riding the fictional horse, Black Bess, from London to York. Turpin would have been probably forgotten had it not been for the romantic embellishments of his villainous deeds.

Address 6 Lead Mill Lane, York, YO1 9QH | Getting there Train to York, then a 10-minute walk | Hours Unrestricted | Tip Visit York Tyburn, site of the hanging gallows that executed Dick Turpin in 1739 (Tadcaster Road, York).

24 Dracula's Birthplace

Romantic views inspired Bram Stoker's dark mind

In 1890, Bram Stoker, author of the 1897 Gothic novel *Dracula*, visited the seaside town of Whitby. Staying at Mrs Veazey's guesthouse at 6 Royal Crescent, Stoker would take strolls and savour romantic seascapes of the picturesque town. Amidst the windswept headland, dramatic abbey ruins, a church surrounded by swooping bats and the town's association with jet (a black, semi-precious stone used in mourning jewellery), Dracula was born in the mind of Stoker.

Stoker visited the library in Whitby and discovered an 1820 book recording a 15th century Moldavian (now in Romania) prince named Vlad Tepes, or 'Vlad the Impaler'. Impaling his enemies on wooden stakes, Vlad was nicknamed Dracula, meaning 'son of the dragon' or 'devil' in the Wallachian language. Stoker began to form his literary ideas. During his visit, Stoker also discovered an 1885 shipwreck of the Russian vessel *Dmitry* from Narva, which ran aground at Tate Sands near Whitby's harbour, carrying a cargo of silver sand. The shipwrecked schooner in *Dracula* became the *Demeter* from Varna that carried Dracula to Whitby, with a cargo of silver sand and boxes of earth.

As Stoker's fictional, undead protagonist reached England's shores, the *Demeter's* crew all dead and her captain lashed to the wheel, an immense black dog was the only survivor. The canine Dracula leapt ashore, ran up the 199 steps towards St Mary's Church and the abbey, and morphed into a blood-sucking, coffin-dwelling, Transylvanian mass murderer. In the graveyard at St Mary's church, there is a real tombstone of a man named Swales. In the novel, Swales becomes Dracula's first Whitby victim. Today, you can sit on the memorial bench and gaze at the panoramic views that inspired Stoker to create Dracula in all his gothic splendour and horror. The bench, erected in 1980 by the Dracula Society, marked the 68th anniversary of Stoker's death.

Address Khyber Pass, West Cliff, Whitby, Yorkshire, YO21 3DQ | Getting there Train to Whitby, then a 12-minute walk | Hours Unrestricted | Tip The Dracula Experience brings the Bram Stoker's novel to life through immersive actor performances in a building once owned by Sir Isaac Newton (9 Marine Parade, Whitby, www.draculaexperience.co.uk).

25 Eden Prisoner of War Camp

Wartime history on display

In 1942, the War Office recognised the need for Prisoner of War (POW) camps to house captured Italian and German military. The first inmates to arrive at Malton were 250 Italian POWs who constructed a permanent camp of 45 huts over 8 acres. The site was designated POW Camp 83 and named Eden Camp, one of 33 camps across Yorkshire and over 400 across Britain.

Prisoners were put to work on farms under the control of the War Agriculture Office. By 1943, Italian soldiers had been relocated, and Eden Camp became home to Polish troops preparing for the D-Day invasion (see ch. 3). The first German POWs arrived in 1944, and the final one left the camp in 1949. German POWs were 'graded' according to their Nazi doctrine and had ID documents assigned to them. Grade A (white) were considered anti-Nazi; Grade B (grey) had less clear feelings; Grade C (black) had probable Nazi leanings; whilst Grade C+ (also black) were deemed ardent Nazis. With fraternisation between low-risk POWs and local people, though, many found friendship and even love and marriage. Though their daily life was not easy, POWs were given food rations and 're-education' programmes to 'de-Nazify' them.

By the 1950s, the camp was used for agriculture and began to fall into disrepair. In 1985, entrepreneur Stan Johnston bought the site, intending for it to be turned into a crisp factory. However, three Italian ex-POWs approached Johnston, and the idea of preserving the site was born. In 1987, Eden Camp opened to the public.

Today, the award-winning attraction has 33 huts, each with a particular wartime theme, including The Blitz, Civil Defence and The Rise of Hitler. The original buildings add a sense of authenticity where social and military history is retold. Displays include military vehicles, air raid shelters, a (dismantled) nuclear bomb and an array of recreated scenes from wartime Britain.

Address Eden Camp, Malton, North Yorkshire, YO17 6RT, +44 (0)165 369 7777, www.edencamp.co.uk, admin@edencamp.co.uk | Getting there Train to Malton, then a 10-minute taxi ride | Hours Daily 10am–5pm | Tip During low tide you can see the wreck of a World War I concrete ship, MV Creteblock, built when steel was scarce (Cleveland Way Trail between Whitby Abbey & Saltwick Bay, Whitby, Yorkshire).

26 — The Halifax Gibbet

"From Hell, Hull and Halifax, good Lord deliver us"

Halifax is a market, mill and minster town that had a particularly harsh way of dealing with petty theft: the guillotine. The 'clean-death machine' is attributed to Joseph-Ignace Guillotin in 1792 during The Terror during the French Revolution. Yet at least 400 years earlier, the folks of Halifax were using a similar device to execute thieves, known as the gibbet. Halifax operated the Gibbet Law – a last vestige of the Anglo-Saxon custom of infangthief, which allowed feudal lords to permit summary justice on thieves within the borders of their fiefdom.

If a felon in Halifax was caught with stolen goods to the value of 13-and-a-half pence, then three market days would pass before he would have his head cut from his body. It is thought that over 100 convicts were beheaded at Halifax from 1286. The Halifax Gibbet consisted of a wooden structure housing an axe-shaped blade on a rope. The blade was rarely sharpened; therefore, often just the sheer weight of the heavy knife crushing the neck of the criminal caused the head to be ripped off. In *The Thieves Lament*, a reference to the harsh punishment states "From Hell, Hull and Halifax, good Lord preserve us." Nearby Hull also had a similar device constructed in the estuary, where convicts were chained and drowned by the rising tide.

The Halifax Gibbet's final victims were Abraham Wilkinson and Anthony Mitchell, both executed in 1650 for stealing 9 yards of cloth. After it was abandoned, Gibbet legislation was superseded by common law of the land. In 1840, the gibbet platform was rediscovered, and a full-sized replica was erected on the original stone base in 1974. The site includes a commemorative plaque bearing names of 52 people known to have been gibbeted here. While the French guillotine was used in a class war, the Halifax Gibbet was used to protect the *haves* against the *have nots*.

Address Bedford Street North, Halifax, West Yorkshire, HX1 5DL, www.visitcalderdale.com/halifax-gibbet | Getting there Train to Halifax, walk to Halifax town centre, take Pellon Lane, turning left onto Bedford Street North | Hours Unrestricted | Tip Milner Field Ruins is a former mansion with a gruesome reputation of death, illness and misfortune. Visit it in Delph Wood, near the main bridle path (Higher Coach Road, Bingley, West Yorkshire).

27 Hillsborough Disaster
'You'll Never Walk Alone'

On 15 April, 1989, the FA Cup football semi-final between Liverpool FC and Nottingham Forest FC was played at Sheffield Wednesday's Hillsborough stadium, chosen as a neutral ground. 53,000 fans headed there to watch the game. During the 1980s, football crowds had a reputation for hooliganism and violence, and team supporters required segregation. Earlier in 1985, during a European Cup final between Liverpool and Juventus at the Heysel Stadium in Brussels, crowd trouble culminated in a surge by Liverpool supporters and left 39 dead.

Against this cultural background, Liverpool fans piled into entrance tunnels at Hillsborough directly into pens. Liverpool was a larger club, but it was allocated the smaller end of the stadium. Common at the time, fans stood on terraces and were separated from the pitch by large perimeter fences. With poor entry control and crowd congestion outside the stadium, fans continued to push forward into the pens in search of space. The influx of people began to cause severe crushing in the pens, as fans began climbing over fences to escape the mayhem. Barriers gave way, and people fell on one another, losing consciousness under the crush. As the match was abandoned, horrors of disaster were played out on live television. The crush resulted in 96 deaths; the youngest victim was Jon-Paul Gilhooley, aged 10. The final victim was in a persistent vegetative state, never regained consciousness, and died in 1993.

Liverpool fans were blamed for the cause of the tragedy. However, after years of legal wrangling, police collusion and mishandling by authorities, Liverpool fans were exonerated in 2016. Numerous memorials exist across Sheffield and Merseyside, including the Hillsborough Disaster Memorial Garden at Hillsborough Park & Walled Garden. This tranquil space offers a reflective place to contemplate the tragedy and its tortuous aftermath.

Address Hillsborough Park & Walled Garden, Parkside Road, Sheffield, S6 4HD |
Getting there Train to Sheffield Interchange, then transfer to bus 57 Stockbridge to
Dykes Hall Road/Middlewood Road | **Hours** Unrestricted | **Tip** There is another
Hillsborough Stadium Disaster Memorial at Sheffield Wednesday FC (92 Penistone
Road North (A 61), Sheffield).

28 Mental Health Museum

Shining light on the darker recesses of our minds

Mental health is a state of wellbeing in which individuals can leverage their own ability to cope with stresses of life. In a modern world that appears to spin ever faster, mental health is increasingly the subject of debates about personal welfare. In bygone years, however, psychological disorders were often considered to be deviant behaviours.

The Mental Health Museum is a unique collection of exhibits and artefacts related to psychology and psychiatry. Spanning the history of mental health care from the early 19th century to the present-day, the museum attempts to raise awareness of well-being and mental health. Look for historic electroconvulsive therapy equipment, chains to restrain patients, and a padded cell, as the museum aims to foster debate rather than offer glorification or titillation.

The museum opened in 1974 as the Stephen G Beaumont Museum at the Stanley Road Hospital in Wakefield. The exhibits focused exclusively on the history of the hospital, which had opened as the West Riding Pauper Lunatic Asylum in 1818 and became the largest mental health provider in Yorkshire. A notable inmate of the original institution was Mary Heaton who, in 1837, was committed for 41 years because she challenged a vicar over an unpaid bill. She suffered horrific, pseudo-scientific experiments there. She died in 1878, aged 77 and was buried in an unmarked pauper's grave. A Blue Plaque unveiled in Wakefield in 2020 recognizes the suffering and injustice she endured.

In 1995, the Stanley Road Hospital was decommissioned, and the Mental Health Museum moved to Fieldhead Hospital. The museum is an affiliate of the 'Happy Museum' scheme, which explores the roles of museums in community health and justice. The Mental Health Museum creates opportunities to challenge stigmas and prejudices of mental illnesses – and to shine light on the darker recesses of our minds.

Address Fieldhead Hospital, Ouchthorpe Lane, Wakefield, West Yorkshire, WF1 3SP, +44 (0)192 431 6360, www.southwestyorkshire.nhs.uk/mental-health-museum/home, museum@swyt.nhs.uk | Getting there Train to Wakefield Westgate or Kirkgate, then various buses towards Fieldhead Hospital, or a five-minute taxi ride | Hours By appointment only | Tip At the Bradford Police Museum, you can discover Britain's criminal justice and civic enforcement heritage (City Hall, Centenary Square, Bradford, West Yorkshire, www.bradfordpolicemuseum.com).

29 — Old Mother Shipton's Cave

A 'witch' who could turn objects to stone

In an unspoilt remnant of a Royal Forest at the end of Sir Henry Slingsby's Long Walk in Knaresborough, is the enchanting place of England's most famous prophetess. Old Mother Shipton's Cave and its Petrifying Well have attracted visitors since 1630, making it the oldest tourist attraction in the country.

In 1488, during the reign of King Henry VII, Agatha Southeil gave birth to a deformed daughter, Ursula. At only 15 years old, Agatha refused to reveal the father and was banished with the child to a cave opposite Knaresborough Castle. Two years later, the Abbot of Beverley took pity, and a local family took in Ursula. Agatha was sent to a convent and never again saw her daughter.

As Ursula grew up, she was taunted for her ugliness. However, at 24 years old, she married Tobias Shipton, a carpenter from York. He died soon after, but Ursula kept his name – the 'Old Mother' title came later in her life. Mother Shipton returned to her cave, foretelling fortunes and predictions. Even the King sent messengers, including Cardinal Wolsey, to hear her prophecies. She is said to have predicted the Plague in 1665, the Great Fire of London in 1666 (see ch. 97) and the defeat of the Spanish Armada. Among her other apparent divinations were the English Reformation, the American Civil War and the French Revolution. Her 'witch-like' reputation was further enhanced by a dropping well near her cave. Dripping water rich in sulphate and carbonate would petrify objects and turn them to stone. Mother Shipton died in 1561, aged 73. With no Christian burial, her grave has been lost to time.

Today, her cave and well remain, and petrified objects, including teddy bears, are on sale at the gift shop. One of Mother Shipton's final prophecies was the world ending 'when the High Bridge is thrice fallen.' The High Bridge at Knaresborough has collapsed twice.

Address Prophecy House, Harrogate Road, High Bridge, Knaresborough, North Yorkshire, HG5 8DD, +44 (0)142 386 4600, www.mothershipton.co.uk, info@mothershipton.co.uk | Getting there Train to Knaresborough, then a five-minute walk | Hours See website for seasonal hours | Tip Spend time in Ripon Cathedral's Crypt, built in 672, which was based on the tomb of Jesus Christ (Minister Road, Ripon, North Yorkshire, www.riponcathedral.org.uk).

30 _ Royal Armouries
State-sponsored shrine for weapons of war

At the heart of a rejuvenated Leeds Docks is the Royal Armouries, a national museum that houses the National Collection of Arms and Armour. The original collection was located within the White Tower, the Norman keep at the Tower of London. As part of Strategy 2000, the purpose-built museum, spread over five floors, opened in 1996 at a cost of £42.5 million. It is home to over 70,000 examples of arms, armour and artillery dating from antiquity to the present-day. The Armouries is also home to one of the largest arms reference libraries in the world.

In the Hall of Steel, the architectural centrepiece of the museum, is the largest mass display of arms and armour created since the 19th century. Other exhibitions include the War Gallery and Oriental Gallery, where arms created in the Middle and Far East were used to extract warfare. The Self-Defence Gallery examines forms of personal protection, including a vampire killing kit, an anti-garrotting Belgian pistol and guns used by fictional 007 spy James Bond. The Make Believe Gallery showcases arms from movies and popular culture, including the Pulse rifle from the movie *Aliens*, an Imperial Stormtrooper blaster from *Star Wars* and swords used in the *Lord of Rings* movie trilogy.

The Peace: Farewell to Arms Gallery is perhaps the most provocative, particularly considering this is a national collection of weapons. On display is body armour famously worn by Princess Diana in 1997 as she toured de-mined areas of Angola. Also on display is the *Chair*, a sculpture made from guns taken out of circulation after the Mozambique civil war. In essence, the Royal Armouries is a state-sponsored shrine to the ways in which monarchs, governments and despots have invented tools to kill one another through the ages. And the exhibitions illustrate the ways many individuals, groups and nations choose to replace conflict with peace.

Address Armouries Drive, Leeds, West Yorkshire, LS10 1LT, https://royalarmouries.org/venue/royal-armouries-museum, enquiries@armouries.org.uk | Getting there Train to Leeds, then a 17-minute walk | Hours Daily 10am–5pm | Tip The Peace Museum is the only museum in the UK dedicated to the history of peace and well worth a visit (10 Piece Hall Yard, Bradford, West Yorkshire, www.peacemuseum.org.uk).

31 Sheffield Cemetery
A park for both the living and the dead

Making dramatic use of a quarried hillside site, the Sheffield General Cemetery opened in 1836 as a response to overcrowding in Sheffield churchyards. Exacerbated by a cholera epidemic in 1832, the cemetery opened as a non-conformist burial ground. In one of the first commercial landscape cemeteries in Britain, Sheffield architect Samuel Worth designed a park for the dead in the Victorian imagination with its Greek Doric and Egyptian style monuments, catacombs and gatehouse. It is also one of the earliest working cemeteries in the country, opening before the *Cemeteries Clauses Act 1847*, and well before its contemporaries including Highgate and Brompton in London.

The first burial was Mary Ann Fish, who died of tuberculosis. The cemetery is also home to the largest grave plot in Britain, holding the bodies of 96 pauper residents. In 1846, an Anglian chapel and consecrated burial ground was added. It was separated from non-conformist graves by the Dissenter's Wall, which partially remains today. Closed for burials in 1978 and containing 87,000 internments, much of the original Anglian burial grounds have been emptied of human remains and landscaped.

Amongst the eternal residents, William Parker's prominent family monument towers above its counterparts. Parker, who died in 1837, was a cutlery pioneer in the 'Steel City' and former Master Cutler of Sheffield. However, it was Parker's wife, Katherine who really suffered. As Parker had died without leaving a will, a destitute Katherine was left with five children, and she hanged herself in 1844. A coroner concluded she had 'immense anxieties and much to manage'. Other notable graves include George Bassett, founder of the confectionery that invented Liquorice Allsorts. Today, the cemetery is a tranquil park and nature reserve that is full of dead local luminaries telling heritage tales.

Address Cemetery Avenue, Sheffield, S11 8NT, +44 (0)114 268 3486, www.gencem.org, sgct@gencem.org | Getting there Train to Sheffield, then bus 4, 65, 81, 82, 83a, 88 or 272 | Hours Daily dawn–dusk | Tip Visit *Women of Steel*, a memorial to the women who kept local steelworks alive during both world wars (Holly Street, Sheffield, S1 2HB).

32 — York Cold War Bunker

Spine-chilling reality of nuclear attack

York has an illustrious history dating back to the Mesolithic people, who settled in the region between 8000 and 7000 B.C. Later, the area was occupied by the Brigantes, an ancient Briton tribe. York was founded in A.D. 71, when the Romans conquered the Brigantes, and has since been at the centre of English history with Viking raids, Norman conquests and medieval monastic legacy. Despite world-renowned buildings and rich cultural heritage, a little known semi-subterranean bunker would have been the last thing standing in York had the Cold War gone hot.

The York Cold War Bunker is located in the Holgate district, a 30-minute walk from the city centre. Surrounded by houses and apartments, the semi-submerged bunker is a remnant of the Cold War. This was the period spanning from 1947 to 1991 of ideological and geopolitical tension between the US and the USSR (and their respective allies) during which numerous proxy wars were fought. Threat of all-out nuclear war, however, was very real, and Britain built a comprehensive network of up to 30 supposedly bomb-proof command and control bunkers. Many of these bunkers are now either in ruins or have been appropriated to other uses. The York Bunker, built in 1961, was home to the regional headquarters of the Royal Observer Corp No. 20 and designed to monitor radioactive fallout in the event of a nuclear attack. During the 1962 Cuban Missile Crisis, the bunker was put on red alert and readied for imminent nuclear attack on the UK.

The spine-chilling reality of nuclear war is brought to life with the 'colour psychology décor' of the bunker, together with 1980s monitoring and communications equipment. Designed to house 60 people, decontamination rooms and sewage ejectors were intended to seal off the bunker from Armageddon. The bunker was decommissioned in 1991 and opened as a tourist attraction in 2006 by English Heritage.

Address Monument Close, York, YO24 4HT, +44 (0)370 333 1181, www.english-heritage.org.uk/visit/places/york-cold-war-bunker, yorkbunker@english-heritage.org.uk | **Getting there** Train to York; bus 1 or 412 to Acomb Road | **Hours** See website for hours and tours | **Tip** Visit the Plague Stones, where supplies were left for York plague victims in 1604 (Little Hob Moor, Tadcaster Road, York).

33 The Disappearing Gun

Built to defend, but never fired in anger

England has a long history of enemy assault arriving by sea. From the Roman conquest of Britain starting AD43 and Viking raids in the Middle Ages, to French, Spanish and Dutch medieval seaborne attacks, to Operation Sea Lion – Hitler's planned invasion of England in 1940 – the sea has brought Britain her foes. So to deter enemy attacks, sea defences are often elaborate and experimental.

The Victorian artillery piece that sits on the headland overlooking the majestic North Sea at South Shields is called the 'Disappearing Gun'. Located at the south end of Longhaven Beach, known locally as Trow Rocks, the weapon seen today is a substitute for the original cannon mounted in 1887 and was installed in 1987. The large artillery gun is 'disappearing' in the sense that its experimental mounting allowed it to be raised and lowered within the 14-foot-wide, concrete gun pit. Using both innovative hydraulic and pneumatic mechanics, the 'floating platform' was also known as the Clarke-Maxim Disappearing Platform, which first appeared in 1885.

The new gun was mounted for practice and used by the Durham Artillery Volunteers, who paid the Tyne Improvement Commissioners for lease of the land. In 1887, the site was loaned to the War Office, but trials of the new gun proved unsuccessful, and the Clarke-Maxim disappearing gun experiment was declared "unlikely to be of any value and no more should be constructed." The gun, designed to hurt and harm enemies and protect against attack, was never fired in anger.

What remains of this 19th century coastal defence technology is a replica gun in the original Grade II Listed fortification. The site was last restored in 2015 by the Territorial Army but has suffered from vandalism over recent years. More recently, the National Trust has bid to restore the structure and conserve its unique status as a visitor attraction.

Address Trow Rocks, Longhaven Beach, South Shields, Tyne & Wear, NE33 2JH |
Getting there Metro to South Shields, then a five-minute taxi ride | Hours Unrestricted |
Tip Immerse yourself in the reconstructed Arbeia Roman Fort (Baring Street, South
Shields, www.arbeiaromanfort.org.uk).

34 Grace Darling Museum
Maritime heroine and reluctant celebrity

The Grace Darling Museum in the seaside village of Bamburgh tells the story of a fearless lady who became a reluctant celebrity. Born in 1815, Grace was the seventh of nine children to William and Thomasin Darling. When Grace was a baby, the family moved to Brownsman Island, part of the Farne Islands off the North Sea in Northumberland, where William was a lighthouse keeper. In 1826, the family moved to a new lighthouse at Longstone, the furthest out of the Farne Islands. Grace soon became an expert of tides and the sea, and she helped her father with lighthouse duties.

On 7 September, 1838, the SS *Forfarshire* suffered boiler problems while sailing to Dundee and ran aground during a huge storm off the Farne Islands. Hurtled against Big Harcar Rock, the steamship broke into two and sank with 35 souls lost. Grace saw the wreck from the lighthouse and set out on a perilous rescue mission with her father, risking their own lives to save others.

Rowing a small coble boat together in mountainous seas, they battled for over a mile to find nine survivors. The survivors included a Mrs. Dawson, who was found clutching her two dead children. Grace and her father rowed back to Longstone with the survivors and cared for them for three days whilst the storm abated.

Capturing the public's imagination, Grace became a national heroine and celebrity, receiving gifts, including £50 from Queen Victoria, and even requests for lockets of her hair. But the attention soon took its mental toll on Grace. With her privacy eroded, Grace withdrew and became ill with tuberculosis. She died in her father's arms on 26 October, 1842, aged 26. She is buried at St Aidan's Church with a memorial opposite the museum, which opened in 1938. Since the Royal National Lifeboat Institution (RNLI) was founded in 1824, its lifeboats and crews have saved over 140,000 lives in British waters. Grace's memory lives on in the RNLI tradition.

Address Radcliffe Road, Bamburgh, Northumberland, NE69 7AE, +44 (0)166 821 4910, www.bamburgh.org.uk/visiting-bamburgh/grace-darling, askgracedarling@rnli.org.uk | **Getting there** By car, take the A1 to B1342 in Bamburgh | **Hours** See website for seasonal hours | **Tip** Stroll through the gardens at Cragside House, the home of modern artillery inventor Lord Armstrong (Rothbury, Morpeth, www.nationaltrust.org.uk/cragside).

35 Heugh Gun Battery

Britain's only land-sea battle in WWI

The Heugh (pronounced 'yuff') Gun Battery is located on the Hartlepool Headland in County Durham. The use of fixed artillery to protect coasts from enemy attack is one of the oldest practices in the history of England's defences. From the 15th century until 1956, when the last gun battery was decommissioned, coastal artillery offered military security and also protected the British Empire's trading routes.

The Heugh Battery was engaged in one of only two battles between Britain's coastal artillery and enemy ships during the 20th century. One of those battles was the first and only action during World War I (the second was in 1942, involving South Foreland Battery at Dover). At 8am on 16 December, 1914, the towns of Hartlepool and West Hartlepool were bombarded by the German Navy. Though the twin towns were defended by the Durham Royal Garrison Artillery, 132 people were killed, including 37 children, and over 200 were injured. The first enemy shell to fall killed infantryman Theo Jones. Germany lost eight sailors. The destruction of homes and buildings in the town left an indelible mark on the local communities. The bombardment remained one of the deadliest attacks until air raids on London by Gotha bombers in 1917.

The Heugh Battery Museum is located at the original artillery site, and the attack is commemorated here every year. A memorial stands at the site, which includes the original earthwork and associated buried ruins of one of the artillery batteries. The museum recalls the Bombardment of the Hartlepools with a recreated Battery Command Post providing a panoramic coastal view. The museum is also home to a parade ground with large artillery and military vehicles, a sizable and eclectic array of armoury and military artefacts, as well as a trench exhibit (see ch. 44). Much of the museum's work is on reconciliation and the total impact of the 1914 bombardments.

Address Moor Terrace, Hartlepool, County Durham, TS24 0PS, +44 (0)142 927 0746, www.heughbattery.co.uk | Getting there Train to Hartlepool and a 10-minute taxi ride | Hours See website for seasonal hours | Tip 'Experience' life and death inside fighting ships at the National Museum of the Royal Navy (Maritime Avenue, Hartlepool, www.nrm.org.uk).

36 John Kirkpatrick

From ship deserter to war hero

John Kirkpatrick was born in South Shields in 1892 and later died an Australian war hero who was all but unknown in his home country. He attended the local Mortimer Road School and had an affinity with animals, having worked with beach donkeys and milk cart horses. Surviving letters suggest he had left-wing political leanings. In one letter, Kirkpatrick writes, 'I often wonder when the working men of England will wake up… what they want in England is a good revolution.' In 1910, Kirkpatrick sailed with the British Merchant Navy from Newcastle-upon-Tyne to Newcastle, New South Wales. He then deserted his ship and went travelling.

In 1914, a homesick Kirkpatrick enlisted as a stretcher bearer in the Australian Army Medical Corps. He dropped his real surname to avoid detection as a deserter and adopted his mother's maiden name, Simpson. Expecting to be posted home to Britain, his unit, 3rd Australian Field Ambulance, was sent to Gallipoli in April 1915. The Gallipoli campaign, ordered by Winston Churchill and spearheaded by Australian and New Zealand troops (ANZACs), was a military calamity. Hundreds of thousands of soldiers were killed, and Gallipoli is forever seared into the collective national identity of Australia and New Zealand. Kirkpatrick escorted the wounded, under heavy fire, from the beaches, where he often whistled and sang. He later found a stray donkey and named it Duffy to help him in his dangerous task. Private Kirkpatrick was killed by a sniper on 19 May, 1915, aged 22. Duffy also died.

Kirkpatrick became an ANZAC legend and symbolises the sacrifice and valour at Gallipoli. He is revered in Australia, but the British Army failed to recognise his heroism, perhaps because he was a ship deserter. The only UK monument to Kirkpatrick is a privately funded statue unveiled in 1988 in South Shields commemorating the 'man with the donkey'.

Address Kirkpatrick Memorial, Ocean Road, South Shields, Tyne & Wear, NE33 2HT |
Getting there Metro to South Shields | Hours Unrestricted | Tip Learn about the
1936 'Jarrow Crusade', a 285-mile protest march to London against poverty and
unemployment at the South Shields Museum & Art Gallery (Ocean Road, South
Shields, www.southshieldsmuseum.org.uk).

37__ The Poison Garden

Plants that kill rather than heal

Alnwick Gardens is adjacent to the imposing Alnwick Castle, the ancient seat of the Duke of Northumberland. Designed originally by Capability Brown in 1750 and opened in 1997 as a 12-acre horticultural attraction by Jane Percy, the Duchess of Northumberland, Alnwick Gardens offers a meandering and magnificent home to the world's largest *tai haku*, or great white cherry orchard, the largest treehouse restaurants and a Grand Cascade comprising 120 water jets. However, within the beauty of this contemporary horticulture lies a garden that can kill.

Behind a black iron gate with skull and crossbones and a sign that reads, 'These Plants Can Kill', is The Poison Garden. This venomous botanical buffet opened in 2005 and is dedicated to floras which are deadly or narcotic. Percy was inspired by the infamous Medici gardens in her reimagination of Alnwick Gardens. The Medici family was a prominent Florentine banking and political dynasty in the 15th century. They used an array of homegrown poisonous plants to kill their enemies and maintain their wealth and influence. Intrigued with the idea that plants could kill instead of heal, Percy's interest in fatal florae includes henbane, opium and hemlock – all used to anesthetize amputees before the advent of anaesthetics. Percy stated, 'What's really interesting is to know how a plant kills you, and how the patient dies, and what you feel like before you die.'

Killer plants in The Poison Garden include *Brugmansia* or 'Angel's Trumpet', that acts as an aphrodisiac before it kills. Other poisonous plants include *Strychnos nux-vomica* (strychnine), *Ricinus communis* (ricin), mandrake and *laburnum*.

Visitors are warned not to touch, taste or smell the plants. The most dangerous plants are kept in cages under Government licence. Their harmfulness and traditional and modern uses make this garden a trip through toxicity.

Address Alnwick Gardens, Greenwell Road, Alnwick, Northumberland, NE66 1HB, +44 (0)166 551 1350, www.alnwickgarden.com, info@alnwickgarden.com | **Getting there** Train to Alnmouth, then bus X-18 | **Hours** See website for seasonal hours. Poison Garden visits by guided tour only | **Tip** Visit Winter's Gibbet, used to display the corpse of William Winter, who was hanged for murdering Margaret Crozier in 1791 (Steng Cross, near Elsdon, Northumberland).

38__St Cuthbert's Relics

A city built around saintly bones

Cuthbert was an Anglo-Saxon monk, bishop and hermit born around A.D. 634 in what was the Kingdom of Northumbria, one of the original kingdoms of Great Britain. Cuthbert became an important medieval saint, and his cult centred on his tomb at Durham Cathedral.

Northumbria, during the Dark Ages, was a violent place, with frequent Viking raids on monasteries. Tensions between paganism and its conversion to Roman and Celtic Christianity provided Cuthbert with missionary work. His asceticism was complemented by his generosity, and he had a reputation for healing. After a monastic career, Cuthbert retired in 676 to Lindisfarne (known as Holy Island) off the coast of Northumbria and lived as a hermit. He died on 20 March, 687 and was buried in a wooden coffin at Lindisfarne.

In death, Cuthbert became a figure for the reformed identity of Northumbria and England, and numerous miracles were attributed to him. In 698, Cuthbert's coffin was opened, and his corpse was found to be perfectly preserved. His incorrupt remains led to Cuthbert's posthumous cultus, and his body parts became saintly relics. After the Danes invaded Lindisfarne, monks fled and took Cuthbert's body with them, wandering about the country for years. Cuthbert became a travelling spiritual icon. His holy relics made leaving home a valid excuse for the medieval pilgrim-tourist. Eventually, Cuthbert was interred in 995 in Durham. In 1093, Durham Cathedral was built with a bejewelled shrine to St Cuthbert. Destroyed during the Reformation, the shrine was replaced in 1542 and remains there today.

Durham became a city of pilgrimage which grew and evolved around a dead man's bones. Today, spiritual pilgrimages continue alongside the secular traveller. The relics and coffin of Cuthbert that inspired a whole city are displayed as part of the 'Open Treasure' exhibition at Durham Cathedral.

Address Durham Cathedral, Durham, DH1 3EH, +44 (0)191 338 7178, www.durhamcathedral.co.uk/visit-us/open-treasure, visitor.desk@durhamcathedral.co.uk | **Getting there** Train to Durham, then transfer to the Cathedral bus | **Hours** Mon–Sat 10am–4pm, Sun noon–4pm | **Tip** See to the 1965 funeral train that carried the body of Winston Churchill on his final journey. It's at the Locomotion Museum (Shildon, County Durham, DL4 2RE, www.locomotion.org.uk).

39___*22 Bees* Mural

Innocence and youth slayed

A radical Islamist terrorist attacked the Manchester Arena on 22 May, 2017 in one of the worst terrorism atrocities ever in the UK. With a shrapnel-laden, homemade bomb, the suicide terrorist murdered 22 people and wounded 139 others following a concert by American singer Ariana Grande. Since the attack, police have revised the number of people to have suffered physical and psychological injuries to 800.

Over half the victims were children or young people; the youngest to die was eight-year-old Saffie Rose Roussos. On what would have been Saffie's 11th birthday, a memorial garden was unveiled at her local primary school. A pink rose created by the Royal Horticultural Society was called 'Saffie' and revealed at the RHS Flower Show in 2018.

In the immediate aftermath of the atrocity, the city's long established emblem – 'the worker bee' – was resurrected to represent the indomitable spirit of the local populace. Originally, the bee symbol was part of Manchester's coat of arms in 1842, when the city was awash with textile mills that were commonly described as 'hives of activity'. People within them were compared to worker bees for their hard work and collaboration. Over time, the icon became obscured in the cityscape. But the bee came alive again after the atrocity, and it was used extensively in the press and social media. The bee also became a popular tattoo, representing peace and togetherness.

Soon after the bombing, *Manchester Evening News* commissioned graffiti artist Russell Meeham (also known as Qubek) to paint *22 Bees*, a huge mural commemorating the victims. Emblazoned on a wall in the Northern Quarter, the bees are pictured swarming around a honey heart, each one representing an innocent victim slayed. Across Manchester, the bee insignia has been lifted from history and now symbolises unity in the face of darkness and acts of evil.

Address 80 Oldham Street, Manchester, M4 1LE | Getting there Train to Manchester Victoria, then walk 20 minutes | Hours Unrestricted | Tip At Out House, public toilets are turned into a hub of evolving street art (Stevenson Square, Manchester).

40 Alan Turing Memorial

'Father of computer science' castrated by the State

On a park bench in Manchester's 'gay village' sits a life-sized memorial to Alan Turing. Considered the father of computer science, Turing worked for the Government Code and Cypher School at Bletchley Park during World War II (see ch. 69). Leading a team of wartime codebreakers, Turing regularly penetrated secret communications of the Axis powers – most notably the German Enigma ciphers. By cracking intercepted coded messages, his 'Turing Machine' enabled the Allies to defeat the Nazis in many battles, including the Battle of the Atlantic. After the war, Turing joined the University of Manchester, where he helped develop the 'Manchester Computers', including the world's first transistorised computer.

In 1952, Turing began a relationship with Arnold Murray, but homosexuality was a criminal offence at the time, and both men were charged with gross indecency. Turing was convicted. To avoid prison, which would have halted work on his beloved computers, Turing opted for probation. Conditional on his probation was to undergo hormonal treatment designed to reduce homosexual libido. The treatment included injections of what was known as stilboestrol – or chemical castration. On 8 June, 1954, Turing was discovered dead apparently from suicide by a cyanide-laced apple that was found half-eaten near his body. He was 41 years old.

Injustices of homosexuality laws are laid bare by Turing's memorial, where State-sponsored bigotry against homosexuals was once the norm. He received an official apology from the UK Government in 2009 and a posthumous pardon from Queen Elisabeth II in 2014. Today, visitors now offer their own deference to a man of intellect but a victim of prejudice. Turing will forever be a gay icon as well as a mathematical genius. Holding an apple in symbolic perpetuity, Alan Turing's memorial now invites you to be a sitting companion on his immortal park bench.

Address Sackville Gardens, Sackville Street, Manchester, M1 3WA, www.manchester.gov.uk, parks@manchester.gov.uk | Getting there Train to Manchester Piccadilly | Hours Unrestricted | Tip The Pankhurst Centre is dedicated to educating visitors and preserving the history of the Women's Suffrage Movement (60–62 Nelson Street, Manchester, www.pankhursttrust.org/pankhurst-centre).

41___All Saints Burial Ground

Encountering 16,000 corpses buried underfoot

Our dead are never far away from us. At first glance, All Saints Gardens adjacent to Manchester Metropolitan University resembles any other small green space. It is a tranquil oasis in a metropolis, where workers and students can relax, chat or just eat lunch. However, few people know that this urban retreat has thousands of bodies buried just beneath. Before the gardens were a municipal hang-out, this location was a cemetery, where an estimated 16,000 corpses still remain underfoot.

The burial ground opened in April 1820 to cater for working-class parishioners of All Saints Church. The first interment was 21-year-old Fanny Knowles, who lived on nearby London Road. Burials then increased substantially in number, but in March 1856 All Saints Burial Ground was partly closed under the direction of the *Burial Act 1853*. By the end of the 19th century, the cemetery had fallen into disrepair and neglect, including flooded and sunken graves. After 25 years of negotiations, it was not until May 1935 that the former burial ground was transformed into a children's playpark. The dead were never exhumed. Up to 30,000 children enjoyed the new park in the first six weeks, and it was described as one of the 'brightest places' in Manchester. Later in the 20th century, the gardens became part of the University campus.

'Encountering Corpses' was a research project led by Manchester Metropolitan University that saw radar scanning of the park and unveiling of the dead below. Art and music exhibitions provided a means to reconnect with the sheer mass of deceased humanity.

Plans are now afoot to recognise officially the burial grounds at the park. Previously, All Saints Burial Ground had been lost to the mist of time, and the dead had remained silent. Today, when you visit the gardens, consider and reflect upon our departed neighbours under the earth, including Fanny Knowles.

Address Grosvenor Square, Manchester, M15 6BH, www.visitmanchester.com | Getting there Train to Manchester Oxford Road | Hours Unrestricted | Tip Visit the Peterloo Memorial, a 19th century massacre in Manchester when the working classes campaigned for industrial reform (Windmill Street & Lower Mosley Street, Manchester, www.peterloomassacre.org/campaign).

42 Barrow's Bombing Blitz
The 'other Blitz' of World War II

The 'Barrow Blitz' is an oft-forgotten episode from World War II and is retold by The Dock Museum. The Blitz, bombing raids by the German Luftwaffe, often focused on major industrial cities, such as London and Coventry. Yet, located on the outskirts of the picturesque Lake District National Park, Barrow was subject to the 'other Blitz', where over 90 people were killed and 531 injured. The main target for German bombing was the Vickers shipyard and engineering works. In September 1940, an incendiary attack on nearby Salthouse killed a five-year-old boy, who became Barrow's first civilian victim. Barrow's terraced houses near to the docks, often referred to as 'Dockers mansions', caught most of the bombing, with a deluge of missiles, incendiaries and high explosives. During the Barrow Blitz, over 10,000 homes were destroyed, obliterating a quarter of the housing stock. As a result, many Barrovians were forced to take refuge in hedgerows and fields outside the town.

Many Barrovians believe the prelude for the bombing raid was in 1936, when the Hindenburg Zeppelin airship made a low pass over the town. Although the Hindenburg claimed it was carrying passengers on a luxury pleasure trip, many believed it was on a pre-war spying mission of naval shipyards. The Hindenburg later caught fire on 6 May, 1937, during a disastrous landing attempt in New Jersey, US, killing 36 people.

Recently, the Daily Express suggested Cumbria was the safest place in the UK to survive an all-out nuclear attack. However, the newspaper neglected to mention the 1940s Barrow Blitz and the fact that Barrow is now home to BAE Systems Maritime, where Royal Navy nuclear submarines are built. Since its inception in the 1870s, this small town and its dockyard on the outer edge of the Furness peninsula have been at the centre of Britain's nuclear arsenal, and Barrow remains a strategic target.

Address North Road, Barrow-in-Furness, Cumbria, LA14 2PW, +44 (0)122 987 6400, www.dockmuseum.org.uk, dockmuseum@barrowbc.gov.uk | Getting there Train to Barrow-in-Furness, then walk 15 minutes | Hours Wed–Sun 11am–4pm | Tip Discover 'secret pencil kits' used by spies and POWs during World War II, made by the Cumberland Pencil Company – at the Derwent Pencil Museum (Southey Works, Keswick, Cumbria, www.derwentart.com).

43 Blackpool Tower Dungeon
Where horrible history comes alive

Blending theatrical performances with special effects, the Dungeon visitor attraction at the famous Blackpool Tower showcases the region's perilous past with a certain amount of gallows humour. In small groups, visitors walk through 11 themed scenes that mix macabre history with melodramatic horror.

Visitors begin with the Descent, a 'medieval lift' that eerily drops to the heart of the dungeon. You then step into the Dark Chapel, where terrified monks tell tales of Viking raids and War of the Roses battles. The Plague Doctor of 1349 then greets you with signs of the Black Death and rotting corpses. Next, the torture chamber of nearby Lancaster Castle waits, as the Torturer makes you abandon all hope. Then, Judge Blackheart rules you guilty and sentences you to the Labyrinth of Lost Souls. Escaping from the Labyrinth, you find yourself at the centre of the Viking Invasion in 866.

Thereafter, you are welcomed to the depths of Skippool Creek, local caves where smugglers once worked and where no one will hear your screams. The Pendle Witches await you (see ch. 58), as witchcraft is rife in the 1600s, when people deemed to be witches were executed. You too have been found guilty of sorcery, and the interactive Drop Dead drop ride will simulate your execution by hanging (minimum person height for the ride is 140cm). Finally, the Red Lion transports you back to a decadent pub of 1896, where local scoundrels and villains tell stories of scandal and shame.

The Blackpool Tower Dungeon is not for the faint-hearted, and it is not historically accurate. Yet it does bring to life people and places that have been lost to time and confronts our morbid past with a sense of exuberance and exaggeration. It purposefully blends the real with the surreal, and taboos from yesteryear are played out as ghoulish visitor experiences. You can find similar Dungeon attractions in London and York.

Address Bank Hey Street, Blackpool, Lancashire, FY1 4BJ, +44 (0)125 362 2242, www.thedungeons.com/blackpool | Getting there Train to Blackpool North, and then a 10-minute walk | Hours See website for hours | Tip Pay a visit to Pendle Hill, which is linked to the notorious witch trials of 1612 (Barley Village, Barley Car Park for Pendle Hill, Lancashire, BB12 9JX).

44 __ Blackpool's WWI Trenches

Practicing along the promenade

The most enduring images of World War I are of brutal trench warfare at the Western Front. Within the hellish trenches and beyond, up to nine million soldiers died and over 37 million casualties were caused by futile and indiscriminate slaughter.

Less well-known are the practice trenches constructed across the UK to train troops and foster camaraderie. Now lost to nature and missing records, these practice trenches survive as archaeological earthworks. However, numerous training trenches have been uncovered, including at Redmires Reservoir, dug by the Sheffield Pals, and at Breary Banks, North Yorkshire, dug by the Leeds Pals. Many of these locally raised units of friends and neighbours fought at the Battle of the Somme in 1916 and suffered massive losses.

Nearly 100 years after being filled in, training trenches were discovered under Watson Park in Blackpool. In 2014, an archaeological team from the University of Salford identified evidence of a buried trench system from an aerial photograph taken in the 1980s. Covering almost two miles, the World War I training trenches were a replica of the Loos and Arras trenches. However in 1916, and in typical Blackpool style as a premier leisure resort, the trenches were turned into a visitor attraction. The entrance fee for visitors was 6p, plus 1p for a guidebook. Wounded soldiers often acted as guides and shared their experiences. Ironically, those visitors enjoyed the trenches as a leisure outing while the carnage of the Western Front was being played out. But money raised from entrance fees went to support a convalescent hospital for wounded soldiers at nearby Squires Gate.

After the armistice, trenches were backfilled, and the site eventually became a small park. Today, you can wander through the park and experience the war heritage that lies beneath.

Blackpool Council

Watson Road Park was the site of WW1 practice trenches modelled upon those of Loos, Flanders. Originally, they were used for military purposes but were opened to the public in June 1916. The intention was to give civilians a better understanding of the new trench warfare. Admission fees were used to fund the King's Lancashire Military Convalescent Hospital on Squires Gate Lane, and patients acted as guides. An archaeological survey of selected areas of the site was carried out in July 2014.

PROMOTING CIVIC EXCELLENCE
BLACKPOOL CIVIC TRUST

Address Watson Road, Blackpool, FY4 2BP | Getting there Train to Blackpool North, then a short walk to Buchanan Street and take bus 7 to Watson Road | Hours Daily dawn–dusk | Tip Enjoy Sir Hiram Maxim's Captive Flying Machines amusement ride at Blackpool Pleasure Beach. Maxim was the inventor of the first portable machine gun used in World War I (525 Ocean Boulevard, Blackpool, www.blackpoolpleasurebeach.com).

45 Bluebird K7

Donald Campbell's tragic quest for speed

Donald Campbell was the ace of World Water Speed Record-breaking of the 1950s and 1960s. This was an age of machines and velocity. Like his father before him, and having broken a number of speed records himself, Campbell forever pushed the tempo. With the dawn of the Space Age, and to keep himself fixed in the public imagination, Campbell turned to supersonic vehicles to propel him ever faster. One such vehicle was Bluebird K7, a jet engine hydroplane designed to thrust Campbell into the record books. Campbell and Bluebird K7 set seven water speed records between 1955 and 1966.

On 4 January, 1967, Campbell brought his aging K7 to Coniston Water for a last bid to break the 300mph water speed record. With an impatient media goading him on, Campbell made a fateful final run. The wash of his previous run had yet to subside fully, and Bluebird's stability began to falter. The hydroplane lifted from the water at over 320mph, somersaulted and plunged into the depths of Coniston Water. Campbell was killed instantly. His reported final words were. 'I'm getting a lot of bloody row in here... I can't see anything... I've got the bows out... I'm going! ...ugh.' His helmet and his teddy bear mascot – Mr Whoppit – were recovered soon after, but Campbell and his beloved Bluebird K7 lay at the bottom of Coniston Water for 34 years.

Bluebird K7 was finally recovered in 2001, and the remains of Campbell were interred in Coniston cemetery. However, Campbell had reportedly believed that 'Skipper and boat stay together'. His daughter, Gina Campbell, gave permission to recover Bluebird, instructing: "Find my dad, so I can put him somewhere warm." Today, the restored, iconic Bluebird K7 has been gifted to the Ruskin Museum, where a special exhibition tells a fatal tale of human adventure to go ever faster in fallible machines.

Address The Ruskin Museum, Coniston, Cumbria, LA21 8DU, +44 (0)153 944 1164, www.ruskinmuseum.com, information@ruskinmuseum.com | Getting there Train to Foxfield or Windermere, then a 20-minute taxi ride | Hours Daily 10am–4.30pm | Tip Adventure at nearby Honister Slate Mine and step across The Infinity Bridge, spanning a gorge 2,000 feet above the valley (Honister Pass, Borrowdale, www.honister.com).

46 _ Captured Africans
Memorial
Trading human cargo

Captured Africans is a memorial and tribute to enslaved Africans who were carried on ships from Lancaster. The slave trade – also known as the 'triangular trade route' or 'Roots Triangle' – saw ships with manufactured goods bound for West Africa from Europe to trade for a cargo of purchased or kidnapped Africans, and then sailed to the Americas, where slaves were sold for raw materials. The ships traveled back to Europe, completing a triangular trade that lasted from the 16th to 19th centuries. It was a brutal system, where millions of African men, women and children were captured and sold as property. Inhumane realities of slavery meant that hundreds of thousands of captives died during enslavement.

Lancaster developed into the fourth largest British slave port, after London, Bristol and Liverpool. Between 1750 and 1790 alone, Lancaster merchants were responsible for the forced transportation of around 29,000 enslaved people. Much of Lancaster's wealth and, indeed, the British Empire's prosperity was built on the back of slavery. However, there has been a *selective amnesia* with recalling slavery heritage in Great Britain. There is a tendency to focus the abolition of the slave trade in 1807 and slavery itself in 1833 (see ch. 62). Yet, millions of slaves led appalling lives to make Britain a superpower. It is important to commemorate not just the abolition of slavery, but also victims of this odious offence.

Captured Africans contemplates our past trading in human cargo. The memorial was proposed by Professor Alan Rice (University of Central Lancashire, Preston) and commissioned as part of the Slave Trade Art Memorial Project (STAMP). Created by artists Kevin Dalton-Johnson and Ann McArdle in 2005, the memorial makes us reflect on the human cost of our shameful slavery heritage.

Address Damside Street, Lancaster, Lancashire, LA1 1AY, www.ageofrevolution.org/
200-object/captured-african | Getting there Train to Lancaster, then walk 15 minutes |
Hours Unrestricted | Tip Visit the Maritime Museum and explore Lancaster's seafaring
slavery history (Customs House, St George's Quay, Lancaster, www.lancaster.gov.uk/
sport-and-leisure/museums/maritime-museum).

47 Carlisle's Cursing Stone

Condemned to the deep pit of Hell

In a gloomy pedestrian underpass near Carlisle's Tullie House Museum, a 14-tonne granite stone is inscribed with 300 words from a 1069-word curse that is thought to be one of the world's longest curses.

Designed by local artist Gordon Young as part of the 2000 Millennium celebrations, the wording is from *The Monition of Cursing* by Archbishop Gavin Dunbar of Glasgow in 1525. This curse was preached from pulpits in the disputed Scottish Borders in order to excommunicate the thieving, murdering, raping and godless Reiver families of the region. The artwork includes an 80-metre path bearing names of the Reivers, and the artist is actually a descendant of one of the families cursed to the "deep pit of Hell, there to remain with Lucifer and all his fellows" unless they ceased their criminal ways and returned to the Church. Dunbar's curse was not the first to be issued against the Reiver families. In 1498, the Bishop of Durham denounced the Reivers of Tynedale for their sinful habits.

In 2005, even though the curse was originally from a holy man, Christian groups and Councillors complained the 'occultist' curse brought them misfortune. They called the artwork a 'shrine for devil worship' and wanted it removed. They even suggested the curse brought foot and mouth disease to the city and wiped out livestock. They blamed the cursing stone for devastating floods, closure of regional factories, the murder of a young boy in a local bakery, and even Carlisle United football team's relegation to a lower league!

Kevin Davies, Vicar of Scotby, stated that the stone "is a lethal weapon [and] its spiritual violence will act like a cancer." Meanwhile, the Bishop of Carlisle advocates for a blessing from the Bible to be added to the artwork. Despite the granite boulder's controversy in the city, the Cursing Stone remains and attracts the morbid and curious.

Address Near Tullie House Museum, Castle Street, Carlisle, CA3 8TP | **Getting there** Train to Carlisle, and then a 10-minute walk | **Hours** Unrestricted | **Tip** At Carlisle Castle, you'll discover past conflicts of the Scottish borderlands (Castle Way, Carlisle, www.english-heritage.org.uk/visit/places/carlisle-castle).

48 The Evaders Garden

Tribute to the French Resistance & Allied escapees

The Evaders Garden at Astley Hall depicts both heroism and sacrifice. An award winning RHS Chelsea Flower Show garden in 2015, it is designed to commemorate World War II escapees – or 'evaders' – and the French Resistance and civilians who helped them to safety.

The French Resistance fought against Nazi occupation and the collaborationist French Vichy regime. Made up of men and women from all socio-economic positions and political leanings of French society, *La Résistance* inspired patriotism as it countered an existential threat to French nationhood. In addition to their guerrilla tactics, Resistance fighters also published underground newspapers, provided intelligence to Allied forces, and maintained escape networks for those trapped behind enemy lines. The Nazis executed many Resistance fighters and civilians. However, the Resistance formally became a part of the French Forces of the Interior (FFI), thus giving France the fourth-largest army by May 1945.

John Everiss, the local man who designed the Evaders Garden, was inspired by his own father Stan, who was an RAF evader himself. Shot down over France on 16 April, 1943, the injured Stan received help to regain his freedom by ordinary French civilians and the Resistance.

The garden design reflects the bond between helper and evader. It features a downed airman forged from slices of rusted steel, his parachute forming part of the path leading into a ruined church. Crouched into a corner, the airman gazes up to a stained-glass window where two French people reach out to help him. The church wall contains names of those who assisted Stan to escape, many of whom were later executed. Engraved on a nearby tombstone is a code poem by Leo Marks, *The Life That I Have*, which was used to encrypt messages in occupied Europe. Mass plantings surround the sculpture, as nature symbolically reclaims the abandoned church.

Address Astley Hall and Park, off Hallgate, Astley, Chorley, Lancashire, PR7 1NP, +44 (0)125 751 5151, www.astleypark.co.uk, astleyhall@chorley.gov.uk | Getting there Train to Chorley | Hours Unrestricted for the park and garden | Tip Astley Hall hosts another important place to remember our war dead in the Garden of Reflection.

49 Grizedale Forest & Hall

Former German POW camp and U-boat Hotel

Grizedale Forest is nestled in the heart of the Lake District National Park. With spectacular scenery and fells, activities range from peaceful walks, to exhilarating mountain bike rides, to adventure courses that send you swinging over the treetops. The forest is also home to unique sculptures that capture the essence of the woodlands. But Grizedale holds a secret of which many are unaware. The former Grizedale Hall was home to German prisoners of war during World War II.

The original Grizedale Hall was built in 1614 by the Rawlinson family. In 1745, Richard Ford built a new mansion house that was demolished in 1904. Once again, the hall was rebuilt by 1907, this time by Harold Brocklebank, a wealthy, Liverpool-based shipping magnate. He lived there until his death in 1936, when the hall and its 4,500-acre estate were taken over by the Forestry Commission. From 1939 to 1946, Grizedale Hall was commandeered by the War Office and became officially known as No. 1 POW Camp (Officers). With watchtowers and double perimeter fences that encircled the hall, the camp held the most elite and senior German POWs.

Prisoners included General Field Marshal Gerd von Rundstedt, thought to be responsible for numerous war crimes but never tried. General Max von Herff was a high-ranking commander in the murderous division of the Nazi Waffen-SS. Many of the POWs captured were German submariners, and the camp, for its relative luxury, became known as 'U-boat Hotel'. Germany's most successful U-boat captain, until his incarceration at Grizedale, was Otto Kretschmer, who had sunk 47 ships and killed thousands of sailors.

In 1957, the hall was demolished, but remains of the wall, gates and stairs of the garden terrace are still visible today at the Yan Visitor Centre. The centre is built on the former Grizedale Hall, and a small exhibition tells the tale of its dark heritage.

Address Grizedale Forest, Ambleside, Cumbria, LA22 OQJ, +44 (0)300 067 4495, www.forestryengland.uk/grizedale | Getting there Train to Windermere, then a 10-mile taxi ride | Hours See website for seasonal hours | Tip Visit the perilous, stone Fairy Steps that were used to transport the dead in their coffins from Arnside to nearby cemeteries (Beetham to Hillcrest Drive, Slack Head).

50 Hack Green Nuclear Bunker

'Protect and Survive' nuclear war

Buried in the peaceful plains of rural Cheshire lies a military bunker designed to 'protect and survive' a nuclear apocalypse. Built in the 1950s as part of a secret radar network codenamed ROTOR, Hack Green would have been the home of the Regional Government had nuclear war erupted. In 1984, the bunker complex went operational as a 35,000-foot nuclear command and control centre for north-west England. With the omnipresent threat of nuclear annihilation during the Cold War, the site was not declassified until 1993.

Opened in 1998 by Rod Siebert, the museum now invites curious visitors to explore an underground labyrinth of Cold War memorabilia and experience a simulated nuclear attack. Hack Green has one of the largest collections of decommissioned nuclear weapons in the world. The museum also houses a Ballistic Missile Early Warning System originally from RAF High Wycombe. Hack Green, with its spooky corridors, also hosts incumbent paranormal tours – buffet included!

The site was previously used as a bombing decoy during World War II in order to protect the nearby town of Crewe and its vital railway junctions. Today, Hack Green sits as a chilling monument to fraught political relationships and a reminder that nuclear Armageddon was never far away. Exhibition cabinets show off gas masks, radiation suits and Geiger instruments, while the medical room shows a bloodied mannequin receiving treatment after a thermonuclear attack. In the background, BBC radio announcements play a haunting soundtrack directing civilians on how to deal with their dead.

A prophetic quote by Albert Einstein displayed on one of the bunker's walls simply states: 'If the next world war is fought with nuclear weapons, the war after that will be fought with bow and arrows.' Thankfully, Hack Green was never pressed into service.

RUSSIAN RADAR SUIT
RADAR PRODUCES HARMFUL, HIGH-FREQUENCY RADIO RADIATION. IF AN ENGINEER WORKED CLOSE TO A RADIATING WORKING RADAR HE WOULD BE KILLED "FRIED TO DEATH" JUST LIKE WORKING INSIDE A MICROWAVE OVEN. THIS SUIT IF YOU LOOK CLOSELY IS INTERWOVEN WITH FINE COPPER THREAD. WHEN CONNECTED TO AN EARTH LEAD THE SUIT WOULD AFFORD SOME PROTECTION TO THE ENGINEER WORKING ON LIVE RADAR EQUIPMENT

Address Hack Green Secret Nuclear Bunker, French Lane End, Cheshire East, CW5 8BL, +44 (0)127 062 9219, www.hackgreen.co.uk, coldwar@hackgreen.co.uk | Getting there As a 'secret location', the site is off the beaten track with no direct public transport. Nearest rail station is Nantwich, then a 15-minute taxi ride. | Hours See website for seasonal hours | Tip The Burma Star Island Memorial commemorates the Burma Campaign during World War II, often referred to as the 'Forgotten War' (Queens Park, Victoria Avenue, Crewe).

51 Huskisson's Mausoleum

First-ever railway casualty

William Huskisson was born in 1770 in Malvern and became a British statesman and financier. He spent his formative years in Paris at the time of the French Revolution, which propelled him into politics. He was a Liberal MP for numerous constituencies, including Liverpool from 1825 until his death in 1830. Huskisson was one of the prime-movers in the creation of the British Empire and advocated free trade.

The first intercity railway, financially backed by Huskisson, opened on 15 September, 1830 between Liverpool and Manchester with a procession of eight trains. The opening ceremony was a considerable event, drawing luminaries from government and industry, including the prime minister, the Duke of Wellington. Huskisson had been diagnosed with strangury (an inflammation of the kidneys), and because of surgery, he was told not to attend the event. He did so nonetheless.

He particularly wanted to make amends with the PM, with whom he had politically fallen out. Huskisson travelled on the Northumbrian locomotive, driven by none other than George Stephenson, known as the Father of Railways. When the train made a stop, Huskisson clambered onto the tracks to find the PM's compartment. On the other track, Stephenson's pioneering Rocket locomotive hurtled towards him. Huskisson, unsteady on his feet, fell into the path of the train and suffered fatal injuries. He was the world's first railway casualty!

He is buried in St James Cemetery, now an urban park, in an extravagant mausoleum. Commissioned by his wife, the Greek Revival memorial designed by John Gibson in 1836 is an adaptation of the Choragic Monument of Lysicrates in Athens. A marble statue of Huskisson, originally located within the mausoleum, is now at the Walker Street Gallery in Liverpool. Ironically, Huskisson's tragic death helped spread news of the novel railway and the idea of rail travel for all.

Address St James Mount & Gardens, St James Road, Liverpool, L1 7AZ,
+44 (0)151 709 6271, www.visitliverpool.com | Getting there Train to Liverpool Central,
then walk up Mount Pleasant and turn right into Hope Street | Hours Daily 6am–10pm |
Tip Tour the Williamson Tunnels, an 1800s subterranean folly associated with a predicted
Armageddon at the Williamson Tunnels Heritage Centre (The Old Stableyard, Smithdown
Lane, Liverpool, www.williamsontunnels.co.uk).

52 International Slavery Museum

Difficult heritage of transatlantic slavery

The International Slavery Museum is located within the Merseyside Maritime Museum at the Royal Albert Dock in Liverpool and is dedicated to the history of transatlantic slavery and its legacy. Through collections and public engagement, the museum explores the impacts of chattel and enslavement.

From around 1500 to the mid-19th century, Liverpool ships transported around 1.5 million Africans enslaved by Europeans and Americans on approximately 5,000 voyages across the Atlantic to work on plantations as forced labour. The triangular trade routes between England, West Africa and the Americas brought great wealth and formed the colonial essence of the British Empire. It also brought death to thousands of Africans. For many years, Britain had a selective amnesia when it came to remembering its collective role in transatlantic slavery. The dominant narrative often revolves around Britain's role in abolishing slavery, rather than focussing on the country's central role. Abolitionists such as William Wilberforce brought about change through the *Slave Trade Act 1807*. However, the abolition of slavery in Britain had perhaps more to do with the increased productivity of waged labour, ship cargo efficiency and declines in plantation profitability.

Today, with increasing awareness of contemporary global slavery, human trafficking, and the Black Lives Matter movement, the International Slavery Museum links Liverpool with its difficult slavery heritage. Opened on 23 August, 2007, the bicentenary of the abolition of the British slave trade, the museum is only yards away from the dry docks where 18th century slave ships were repaired and fitted out. Visitors can explore our past slavery roots and to learn how global slavery is still practiced illegally today.

Address Royal Albert Dock, Liverpool, L3 4AQ, +44 (0) 151 478 4499, www.liverpoolmuseums.org.uk/international-slavery-museum | **Getting there** Train to Liverpool Central, then a 20-minute walk | **Hours** Tue–Sun 10am–6pm | **Tip** Visit Church of St Luke, the 'Bombed Out Church', which was gutted during the Liverpool Blitz and left destroyed in honour of the dead (Leece Street, Liverpool, www.slboc.com).

53 IWM North
Stories of war

The proposal for a national war museum by Sir Alfred Mond was accepted by the War Cabinet on 5 March, 1917. The idea was to collect evidence of the Great War, even though it was still ongoing, and record contributions made by all sections of society. A small team of staff was attached to General Headquarters on the Western Front, tasked with gathering material for the museum collections. The original museum in London opened in 1920.

The IWM North opened in 2002 (the term 'imperial' reflects military sacrifices of India and the Dominions). Overlooking the Manchester Ship Canal, it is located at the site of the former Hovis Grain Silos, which were destroyed during the 1940 Manchester Blitz that killed 684 people. The imposing, if not daunting, IWM North building was designed by internationally acclaimed architect Daniel Libeskind, who also designed the masterplan for the new World Trade Center in New York.

IWM North is one of five branches of the Imperial War Museum. The museum charts emotional, political and socio-cultural impacts of war on people and society during the 20th century and onwards. With permanent and temporary exhibitions, artefacts and displays, and award-winning immersive experiences, IWM North narrates stories of suffering on battlefields as well as on home fronts.

Libeskind, whose relatives were murdered during the Holocaust, wanted the building to reflect the globe shattered into three pieces. This represents a post-conflict world put back together but never the same again. Symbolizing war destruction, the building comprises three interlocking 'shards' denoting earth, water and air – each representing battles fought on land, sea and in the skies. With the building purposely disorienting, Libeskind said he sought to 'create a building… which emotionally moved the soul of the visitor toward a sometimes-unexpected realization.'

Address Trafford Wharf Road, The Quays, Stretford, Manchester, M17 1TZ, +44 (0)207 416 5000, www.iwm.org.uk/visits/iwm-north | Getting there Train to Manchester Piccadilly or Victoria, then MetroLink to Harbour City or MediaCityUK | Hours See website for seasonal hours | Tip Make a point of visiting all of the Imperial War Museums: IWM London, Churchill War Rooms, HMS Belfast (all central London based), and IWM Duxford (near Cambridge, www.iwm.org.uk).

54 Lancaster Castle & Prison

Crime, witches and (in)justice

Owned by Her Majesty Queen Elizabeth II (Duke of Lancaster), Lancaster Castle and Prison has witnessed historical, cultural and political trauma over the past 1,000 years. The castle was home to the Lancashire Assizes, known since 1972 as a Crown Court, and is still operational today. Lancashire Assizes had a reputation of passing the death penalty more than any Assize in England. Established in Norman times, the castle stands on an ancient Roman fort, which served as a bastion against marauding Picts. Over the centuries, the castle has incarcerated felons from murderers to cattle rustlers, and been the site of many executions.

The infamous 'Lancashire Witch Trials' in 1612 saw 10 people convicted of witchcraft and hanged on the moor above the town (see ch. 68). Between 1782 and 1865, around 265 convicts were publicly hanged at Lancaster, with spectators thronging 'Hanging Corner'. The unconsecrated dead were buried in castle grounds, without grave markers – and reportedly still remain! In 1865, Stephen Burke was hanged for the murder of his wife, and became the last public execution at the castle. The *Capital Punishment Amendment Act 1868* ended public executions in Britain, and criminals were required to be put to death in private.

The hanging of Thomas Rawcliffe, another wife-murderer, in 1910 was the last ever execution and the prison closed in 1916. During World War I, the castle interned German civilians and prisoners of war. Reopened as HM Prison Lancaster in 1955, the castle was often used for high-security trials until 2011, when it finally closed as Europe's longest-serving operational prison.

The castle is now open for guided tours and incorporates the hanging room, 19th century cells, Crown Court, as well as the former A-wing. With tales of torture and executions, Lancaster Castle and Prison is a 'living monument' to our oft-dark penal history.

Address Lancaster Castle, Castle Parade, Lancaster, LA1 1YJ, +44 (0)152 423 7310, www.lancastercastle.com, info@lancastercastle.com | Getting there Train to Lancaster, then walk 10 minutes | Hours See website for seasonal hours and tours | Tip Visit the Judges Lodgings Museum, home to Thomas Covell, Keeper of Lancaster Castle and notorious 'witch hunter' in the 17th Century (Church Street, Lancaster, www.lancashire.gov.uk).

55 Lost Beatle Bench

Place of pilgrimage for the 'Fifth Beatle'

Regarded as the most influential band of all time, The Beatles were formed in Liverpool in 1960. John Lennon, Paul McCartney, George Harrison and Ringo Starr revolutionised many aspects of the music industry. Originally, however, the 'Fab Four' were, in fact, five members. Stuart Sutcliffe, the 'Fifth Beatle', is often lost from music memory.

Sutcliffe was born in Edinburgh in 1940 and moved to Liverpool as a baby. After attending Prescot Grammar School, Sutcliffe enrolled at the Liverpool College of Art. A highly talented artist, he excelled in the visual arts. During his studies, he worked as a 'bin man' for Liverpool Corporation refuse department.

It was at college that he met John Lennon, and the two formed a strong friendship. In May 1960, Sutcliffe joined Lennon, McCartney and Harrison as a bass guitarist. Though often credited with giving the band its name, Sutcliffe's guitar playing style was elementary, and he appeared uncomfortable on stage. During a tour in Hamburg, Sutcliffe met Astrid Kirchherr, and they became engaged. Deciding to stay in Germany to pursue art, he left the Beatles in July 1961 and enrolled at the University of Fine Arts of Hamburg. Under the tutelage of Eduardo Paolozzi, one of the pioneers of pop art, Sutcliffe is described as one of his best students.

Sutcliffe began suffering from severe headaches and light aversion. Without a proper diagnosis of the headaches, Sutcliffe collapsed on 10 April, 1962 and suffered a cerebral haemorrhage and ruptured aneurysm. He died aged 21 years old. John Lennon went on to describe Sutcliffe as '[my] alter ego [and] a spirit in his world'. Stuart Sutcliffe has been referred to as the 'lost Beatle'. He is buried in Huyton Cemetery, where a memorial bench was unveiled in 2015. The bench was featured in Historic England's 'Immortalised' exhibition of oft-forgotten memorials in 2018.

Address Huyton Parish Church Cemetery, Stanley Road, Liverpool, L36 7SA, +44 (0)151 233 3000 | Getting there Train to Huyton, then walk nine minutes | Hours Mon–Sat 7.45am-10pm, Sun 8.30am–8.30pm | Tip Inside Liverpool Metropolitan Cathedral, you can explore the Lutyens Crypt, with its unusual brickwork (Mount Pleasant, Liverpool, www.liverpoolmetrocathedral.org).

56 Lowther Castle & Gardens

Site of a secret weapon of war

Since the Middle Ages, Lowther Castle in the Lake District National Park belonged to the Lowther family, latterly the Earls of Lonsdale. Mary, Queen of Scots visited Lowther in 1568 as part of her confinement by Queen Elisabeth I. George Macartney, a colonial diplomat, declared in 1793 that Lowther 'might be rendered by a man of sense, spirit and taste, the finest scene in the British dominions.'

Yet Lowther holds a once-classified secret. After the castle closed in 1937, due to the extravagance of Hugh Cecil Lowther, the 5th Earl of Lonsdale, it was requisitioned by the War Office. The 11th Royal Tank Regiment trained at Lowther Castle in clandestineness with a new, secret weapon of war known as the Canal Defence Light (CDL). Using powerful carbon-arc searchlights mounted onto tanks, the CDL allowed troops to target enemy positions. Importantly, the CDL also dazzled and disoriented enemy troops, preventing accurate return fire. Tanks' turrets were replaced with cylindrical ones containing a 13-million-candlepower searchlight and machine gun. General Eisenhower and Winston Churchill both visited Lowther to witness the CDL. But despite 497 American and British tanks being fitted with CDL, it was only used in conflict at the Battle of Remagen in 1945.

After the war, the Lowther family faced crippling debts. In 1947, the castle was put to auction with no buyers. So Lancelot Lowther, the 6th Earl, decided to sell the family silver and stripped the castle, removing roofs and walls. After returning from the War, the final resident, James Lowther, declared that Lowther 'exemplified gross imperial decadence during a period of abject poverty.' Damaged by the army and abandoned to become a pig farm, Lowther Castle became a ruin. Then, in 2011, Lowther Castle reopened as an award-winning destination, with exhibitions, a café, and extensively restored gardens.

Address Lowther Castle, Lowther, Cumbria, CA10 2HH, +44 (0)193 171 2192, www.lowthercastle.org, info@lowthercastle.org | **Getting there** Train to Penrith, then a brief taxi ride | **Hours** See website for seasonal hours | **Tip** A five-minute walk from Lowther Castle is the Lowther Mausoleum at St Michael's Church, resting place of William Lowther, 2nd Earl of Lonsdale, (1787–1872) (www.mmtrust.org.uk/mausolea/view/40/Lowther_Mausoleum).

57 Mexico Lifeboat Tragedy

Worst-ever RNLI disaster

Gazing out across the Irish Sea at St Annes and standing high on a pedestal is a life-sized figure of a lifeboat man. This Grade II Listed sandstone monument commemorates the worst ever disaster for the Royal National Lifeboat Institution (RNLI).

On 9 December, 1886, the German cargo barque *Mexico* left Liverpool to sail to Guayaquil in Ecuador. During a violent storm, fearing sandbanks at the River Ribble estuary, the captain sent out an SOS. The Southport, St Annes and Lytham lifeboats all answered the call. The *Eliza Fernley* from Southport was the first to respond but capsized upon reaching the ship and lost 14 of the 16 crew. Next, the *Laura Janet* lifeboat set out from St Annes but never reached its destination. It was found the morning after, and only three dead bodies of the crew were recovered. The rest were lost to the deep.

The *Charles Biggs* lifeboat from Lytham successfully saved the 12 crewmen of the *Mexico*. With 27 souls lost, 16 widows and 50 orphans were left behind. The incident was a national tragedy for Victorian England. To raise money for families and to fund memorials, the RNLI inaugurated public fundraising with its 'flag days' which continue to this day. Queen Victoria and Kaiser Wilhelm were initial donors.

Unveiled in 1888, the St Annes Lifeboat Memorial remembers the gallantry of local men, including 19-year-old James Harrison, who was aboard the *Lara Janet* and is buried in Layton Cemetery in Blackpool. Other memorials commemorating the tragedy are located in Lytham and Southport.

Britain is an island nation yet still does not have a government-funded lifeboat service. Founded in 1824 by Sir William Hillary, the RNLI is a charity that is principally funded by voluntary donations and legacies. With over 40,000 volunteers and an annual budget of £148m, the RNLI is our often unrecognised 4th emergency service.

Address South Promenade, St Annes-on-the-Sea, Lancashire, FY8 1LW, www.visitstannes.info | Getting there Train to St Annes | Hours Unrestricted | Tip Visit the Old Lytham Lifeboat House, once home to the *Charles Biggs* lifeboat, now a funeral parlour, at Lytham Windmill Museum (Lytham Green, East Beach, Lytham St Annes, www.lythamwindmill.co.uk).

58 The Pendle Witches

Witchcraft and 'ritual magic'

King James VI of Scotland (who later was also James I of England) was convinced witches were plotting against him. In 1597, the king published *Daemonologie,* a book in which he explored necromancy, demonology, and ancient black magic. It was a time of political fear combined with fervent religious bigotry, which often pitted Catholic and Protestant communities against one another. It was also a time of superstition, and tales of ritual magic were used to spread dread of demonic possession.

Against this social backdrop, the Lancashire Witch Trials in 1612 became one of the most influential judgements in English cultural history. In the shadow of the foreboding Pendle Hill, 11 'Pendle Witches' (nine women and two men) were tried for supernatural witchery. The accused were mainly from two families – named Demdike and Chattox – which meant family members testified against one another. Other people were brought into the affray, including Alice Nutter, a young comparatively wealthy woman who was executed on the testament of a nine-year-old child. At the time, individuals used 'witchcraft' to persecute one another because of jealousy, or they were in competition, all trying to make a living from healing, begging, or extortion.

Of the 11 people tried, nine were hanged together at Lancaster Castle and one at York, and the other found not guilty. Three other women known as the 'Samlesbury Witches' were acquitted. Official proceedings by the court clerk, one Thomas Potts, in his *Wonderfull Discoverie of Witches in the Countie of Lancaster* ensured these were the best recorded trials of the 17th century. Alice Nutter is now commemorated as a statue in shackles, as she leaves her home village of Roughlee on her way to the Lancaster gallows. She resembles a woman of her times, someone who pleaded not guilty to witchcraft yet was subject to zealous judgement.

Address Blacko Bar Road, Roughlee, Lancashire, BB9 6NS | Getting there Train to Nelson, then a 10-minute taxi ride | Hours Unrestricted | Tip In nearby Colne Cemetery is the grave of Wallace Henry Hartley, the bandmaster and violinist who played on as the Titanic sank in 1912 (Keighley Road, Colne, BB8 0LS).

59 Preston's Martyrs

Dying for social justice

Economic depression in the early 1840s culminated in the 1842 General Strike, often referred to as the Plug Plot Riots. Spreading to mill towns in the north of England, strikes were influenced by the Chartist Movement and the petition for greater democracy. While women's suffrage is well documented, little is recalled of men's suffrage. Before 1832, very few people had the right to vote, and pressure for parliamentary reform had been building during the 19th century. The Reform Acts of 1867 and 1884 satisfied some moderate reformers. However, it was not until 1918 that all men could vote and 1928 for all women.

Britain managed to introduce voting reform rather than violent revolution. However, working class disenfranchisement resulted in civil unrest. Government rejected the 1838 People's Charter and its fair pay protocol, and disputes intensified. In Preston, a strike started on 12 August, 1842, with 3,000 cotton workers at Chadwick's Orchard (now Preston Covered Market) protesting for social and industrial reform. With more factories joining, a crowd assembled in front of the Corn Exchange Building (now home to 1842 Restaurant & Bar). Men, women and children confronted authorities by throwing stones. Mayor Samuel Horrocks read the *Riot Act 1714*, permitting the use of force to disperse the crowd. Soldiers from the 72nd Highlanders opened fire, killing four men and critically injuring three others. Bernard McNamara was the youngest to die, aged 17.

Despite national outrage, a subsequent inquest ruled the deaths were justified homicide. In 1992, a memorial to the Preston Martyrs, designed by Gordon Young, was unveiled at the site where the shooting took place. Inspired by Goya's 1808 painting *The Third of May*, in which Spanish civilians are executed for resisting Napoleon's troops, the memorial is a stark reminder of sacrifices made for social democracy and fairness.

Address Martyrs Memorial, Lune Street, Preston, Lancashire, PR1 2NN | Getting there Train to Preston, and then walk north on Fishergate Street and turn left into Lune street | Hours Unrestricted | Tip Stop in for a bite at The Crypt, the UK's first-ever horror-themed tea room (31 Birley Street, Blackpool, www.thecryptblackpool.com).

60 Remembering Kitty Breaks

Sand dunes killing

On Christmas Eve 1919, Kitty Breaks was found dead among the windswept sand dunes of St Annes-on-the-Sea. She had been shot three times in the head and had cuts to her leg from fighting her assailant. A Webley service revolver, a pair of men's gloves and a letter from one Frederick Holt were found with her body.

Originally from Bradford, 26-year-old Breaks was married when she met and fell in love with 32-year-old Holt at a Hydro hotel in 1918. Holt, who was a lieutenant with the 4th Royal North Lancashire Regiment, had been invalided out of the army in 1915. Suffering from shell-shock and amnesia, Holt lived off his inheritance in the affluent district of Fairhaven. He had persuaded Breaks to take out life insurance and make a will naming him as her beneficiary. When police arrived to arrest Holt at a hotel in nearby Lytham, he asked whether he could finish his coffee first.

Bloodied footprints found in the sand matched Holt's boots. Gunsmiths traced the revolver back to Holt, and the gloves found near Breaks matched a pair owned by him. During his trial, Holt appeared to be oblivious of his surroundings and his fate. He claimed that the police had tried to kill him using mad dogs, germ-carrying fleas and gas. His defending barrister Sir Edward Marshall Hall argued he served his country gallantly and, as a result of his war injuries, had become insane. Insanity was rejected, and Holt was found guilty of murder, with a probable motive of inheriting life insurance. He was sentenced to death, and on 13 April, 1920, Holt was hanged at Manchester's Strangeways Prison.

No memorial exists today, but the dunes carry her memory. She was immortalised in *Kitty Breaks,* a 2018 song by Lancashire-based folk band Phantom Voices, as a 'ghost wandering a seaside town'.

Address Clifton Road North, St Annes-on-the-Sea, Lancashire, FY8 2LZ | Getting there Train to St Annes, and then a short walk | Hours Unrestricted | Tip You can see the shipwreck Abana at low tide, where the crew mistook Blackpool Tower for a lighthouse in 1894 (Little Bispham Beach, Queen's Promenade, Blackpool).

61 Rock-Tombs of Heysham
The 'Viking Graves'

Overlooking a windswept Irish Sea in the ruins of St Patrick's ancient chapel, close to St Peter's Church in historic Heysham, is a collection of Anglo-Saxon stone graves. Dating from the 10th century and hewn from solid rock, these open sarcophagi bear witness to a funerary practice from long ago. Often filled with rainwater, the six rock-cut tombs invite visitors to peer into resting places of the dead. With an imposing seascape as a backdrop, this Grade II Listed Scheduled Ancient Monument provides a tangible link to our own sense of mortality.

Pilgrims of the past have paid homage to this site for centuries, venerating St Patrick, who was reported to have run aground on Heysham shores. However, St Patrick probably never visited the place, but that does not stop a good story! Yet the bones of the deceased are long gone and their names and lives forgotten to the mist of time. What is left are some of the finest relics of early Christianity in North West England.

The tombs are cut into a large block of flat sandstone rock – four of them body-shaped, the other two with straight sides. At the head of the graves is a small hole, thought to be a socket where timber crosses were placed to mark the burial. An associated cemetery near the rock tombs was excavated in the 1970s, and bones discovered there dated to the 10th and 11th centuries.

Once featured on a Black Sabbath album cover, and known locally as the 'Viking Graves', there is speculation about who was laid to rest in such a spectacular setting. Some argue it was priests of St Patrick's chapel or high-status individuals. Other people argue the tombs were repositories for body parts or saintly relics, rather than for whole corpses. Whatever the case, with a panoramic vista of the Lake District National Park, these 'tombs with a view' remind us of how our ancestors dealt with their dead of stature.

Address St Patrick's Chapel, 1-3 Main Street, Heysham, Morecambe, LA3 2RN, www.visitnorthwest.com/sights/st-patricks-chapel | Getting there Train to Heysham Port, then a 10-minute taxi ride | Hours Unrestricted | Tip Ashton Memorial is a spectacular neo-Baroque folly built by Lord Ashton in memory of his wife (Williamson Park, Williamson Road, Lancaster, www.lancaster.gov.uk/sites/williamson-park).

62 __ Sambo's Grave

A lonely tomb from Britain's slavery heritage

There is a poignant and emotive reminder of Lancashire's involvement in the slave trade of Britain: Sambo's Grave. In an open meadow on the windswept peninsula overlooking Morecambe Bay, near the hamlet of Sunderland Point, is the burial site of an enslaved cabin boy. Up until the 18th century, Sunderland Point was a thriving seaport serving nearby Lancaster. The British Empire undertook trade with Africa and the West Indies, mainly in cotton, rum, sugar – and humans.

Sambo, it is thought, was a young man from Africa taken into captivity by either a sea captain or a merchant. The manner of his untimely death in the 1730s is subject to speculation, but one romantic theory is that Sambo's 'master' was called away on urgent business. Leaving Sambo to wait on the shores of Morecambe Bay, the master never returned, and Sambo, fearing abandonment forever in an alien land, died of a broken heart. Of course, we will never know how or why Sambo died. Resting in unconsecrated ground on the weather-beaten shores of the Irish Sea, his grave was marked by a simple wooden cross.

The splendid isolation of the tomb soon drew curious visitors, including Reverend James Watson, who came to the site in 1795. Entranced by Sambo's story and the aura of the place, Watson collected a shilling from visitors. With the money, he bought a proper memorial stone, complemented with an inscription and a heart-felt poem. Today, you can visit Sambo, read Watson's poem on his grave, and pay homage to his life. But while doing so, do remember the stain of Britain's slavery heritage and its human cargo. Sambo's Grave is now kept adorned with coloured stones and loving mementos from local schoolchildren. Combined with a melancholic seascape, tidal marshes and rural idyll, the atmospheric location of the grave is popular with ramblers, wildlife enthusiasts and artists alike.

Address The Lane, Sunderland, Morecambe, LA3 3HS | Getting there By car, take the single-track road from Overton 1.5 miles to the gravesite. There is a small car park at Sunderland Point. | Hours Unrestricted | Tip Take a moment to enjoy the views from Sunderland Point. But beware: Access is by a single causeway that is cut off at high tide. To avoid being stranded by the sea, check the local tide times (www.tide-forecast.com/locations/Sunderland).

63 Spitfire Memorial
Symbol of sacrifice and a killing machine

Flying high on top of a pole and plinth in Lytham St Annes is a full-sized replica of a Spitfire W3644. The iconic World War II plane set within parkland adjacent to Fairhaven Lake is close to the beaches of the Fylde coast. Its official title is the Lytham St Annes RAF Fighter, Bomber & Coastal Command Memorial.

The Spitfire Memorial was unveiled in 2012, with commemorative plaques honouring RAF, Commonwealth and US Army Air forces. In 1941, Lytham St Annes residents raised £6,500 (over £330k at modern value) to 'sponsor' the original Spitfire W3644. The pilot was Sergeant Alan Lever Ridings, who had family connections with the town. The idea of 'purchasing' a Spitfire during the war was a homefront phenomenon at the time, one that is often forgotten today. Since its launch in 1938, the Spitfire has inspired movie star-style attention, overshadowing the Hurricane fighter. Over £13m (£650m today) was raised through Spitfire funding, and sponsorship became an essential part of the war effort. However, Spitfire W3644 was shot down over Devon in 1942 after escorting bombers over France. The airfields at nearby RAF Stanley Park (now Blackpool Zoo), RAF Squires Gate (now Blackpool Airport), and Warton Aerodrome (now British Aerospace Systems) all played crucial roles in training RAF pilots, hosting US air forces and protecting Liverpool and the Irish Sea.

The Spitfire was designed to kill. With its powerful Merlin engines and lethal machine guns that could deliver 160 rounds per second, the plane was a state-built killing machine. Around 12,000 German fighter pilots were killed during the war. Yet the Spitfire is a cultural, Churchillian symbol of victory rather than of victimhood. The plane is part of our collective national psyche for the bravery and sacrifice of its many pilots, including 544 RAF pilots killed in the 1940 Battle of Britain (see ch. 79).

Address Lytham St Annes Spitfire Memorial, Fairhaven Lake, 211 Inner
Promenade, St Annes-on-the-Sea, FY8 1BD, www.spitfiredisplayteam.co.uk,
john@spitfiredisplayteam.co.uk | Getting there Train to Andsell, and then a 14-minute
walk | Hours Unrestricted | Tip Visit Hangar 42, home to Hawker Hurricanes, Spitfires
and other World War II aircraft vehicles. Open first Sunday of the month, Mar–Nov
10am–4pm (Blackpool Airport, Squires Gate, Blackpool).

64 Titanic in Liverpool
The 'unsinkable ship' that sunk

On 14 April, 1912, RMS *Titanic* struck an iceberg in the North Atlantic on her maiden voyage from Southampton to New York. Over 1,500 souls were sent to the deep, including 59 children. The tragic tale is retold at the Merseyside Maritime Museum in Liverpool. The museum highlights original artifacts, including victims' possessions and keepsakes. Salvaged ceramics from the ship's upper-class restaurants are historical remnants of social class, as well as fragments of fatality.

Titanic never visited Liverpool, but the headquarters of White Star Line, its managing company, was based in the city, and the ship showed 'Liverpool' on its stern. Over 90 crew members came from Liverpool, including Fred Fleet, who first spotted the infamous iceberg. Fred Clark, the bass violinist who hauntingly played as the ship sank, and Chief Officer Henry Wilde also hailed from Liverpool.

Most of White Star's profits came from 'steerage' immigrant passengers, but class distinctions were perpetuated even in death. While lifeboat capacity and design flaws were the primary causes of loss of life, 76 per cent of third-class passengers perished, while 61 per cent of first-class travellers survived. Following the disaster, the CS *Mackay-Bennett* sailed to collect corpses, but the ship soon ran out of coffins. First-class passengers identified by fancy clothes were given valuable coffin space and brought ashore for burial. Second-class passengers were stored in cloth sacks, whilst 'third-class bodies' were buried at sea.

The *Titanic* exhibition in Liverpool contributes to a disaster romanticised in popular culture and adds to Liverpool's sense of 'place-making'. Yet, in reality, the tragedy caused a collapse in confidence of modernity. It revealed our frailties and errors, despite a belief in technological infallibility. *Titanic* is a real-life morality drama about the dangers of human hubris.

Address Merseyside Maritime Museum, Royal Albert Dock, Liverpool, L3 4AQ, +44 (0)151 478 4499, www.liverpoolmuseums.org.uk/maritime-museum | Getting there Train to Liverpool Central | Hours Wed–Sun 10am–6pm | Tip Visit 30 James Street, the former HQ of Titanic's White Star Line and now an iconic hotel (30 James Street, Albion House, Liverpool, www.30jamesstreetliverpool.co.uk).

65 Undamaged Red Post Box

Marker of atrocity and symbol of resilience

An unlikely memorial stands in the centre of Manchester and is testament to community resilience. The Undamaged Red Post Box remained almost unscathed after an Irish Republican Army (IRA) terrorist attack on 15 June, 1996. When the IRA planted a 3,300-pound bomb in a truck and exploded it outside the Manchester Arndale shopping centre, the nearby post box survived. The mail inside the box, still intact, was delivered after the attack. The post box has since become a small but mighty symbol of resilience in the face of political discord and terrorism.

The IRA gave a 90-minute warning to authorities, but bomb disposal units were unable to defuse the device. The explosion destroyed much of the retail area of Manchester, and it was the biggest explosion since World War II. Over 200 people were injured by the detonation, and 75,000 people were evacuated. An estimated 400 businesses within half a mile of the blast were affected, and 40 per cent never recovered from it. While the attack was one of the most expensive man-made disasters ever, it proved to be a catalyst for urban regeneration and investment. Greater Manchester Police announced in 2006 there was no realistic chance of convicting those responsible, and no one has ever been held accountable. Instead, the attack has morphed into yet another of many terrorist atrocities from 'The Troubles', the ethno-nationalist period of conflict in Northern Ireland that lasted from the early 1960s to the late 1990s.

The red pillar post box is an iconic British cultural symbol. Originally painted green until 1874, the Royal Mail adopted red as the standard colour as people had kept walking into them. Made of cast iron, the Undamaged Red Post Box was repaired in 1999 with a bronze commemorative plaque. Today, the post box stands as a marker of atrocity but also as a sign of urban regeneration and community renewal.

Address 15 Corporation Street, Manchester, M1 1PN | Getting there Train to
Manchester Victoria, and then a short walk | Hours Unrestricted | Tip Visit the Peace
Centre, a living memorial to 30-year-old Johnathan Ball and 12-year-old Tim Parry, both
killed in the 1993 IRA bombing of Warrington (Peace Drive, Warrington, Cheshire,
www.thepeacecentre.org.uk).

66 — Western Approaches HQ

Protecting against the U-boat peril

In 1941, Winston Churchill instructed the Headquarters of Combined Operations, later known as The Western Approaches HQ, to be relocated from Plymouth to Liverpool. The wartime unit responsible for monitoring deadly German submarines (or U-boats) in the Atlantic had become vulnerable to enemy attack. Adolf Hitler suspected that headquarters had been moved to Liverpool, which was the main convoy port of Britain (over 1,000 convoys docked there). The heavy bombardment of Liverpool is in part credited to the Luftwaffe's attempt to destroy the headquarters.

The Western Approaches HQ comprised Royal Navy, Royal Marines and RAF personnel. They occupied a 100-room underground bunker beneath Derby House in Liverpool. Covering 55,000 square feet, the bunker was bomb- and gas-proof and was referred to as the 'Citadel' or 'Fortress'. With the threat of U-boat 'wolf-packs' sinking Allied supply ships in the eastern Atlantic, Britain was in danger of starving to death.

On 6 March, 1941, Churchill coined the phrase, 'Battle of the Atlantic', deliberately echoing the 1940 airborne Battle of Britain to emphasise its importance (see ch. 79). The battle was the longest campaign of World War II. Churchill later declared, 'The only thing that really frightened me during the war was the U-boat peril.' With a convoy escort system to protect merchant shipping, Western Approaches HQ and its commander, Admiral Sir Max Horton, were instrumental in defeating the U-Boat menace and winning the Battle of the Atlantic.

Today, the Western Approaches HQ is an engaging museum that recalls this history, and a top-secret bunker is opened up for the war tourist's inspection. Almost 4,000 people died from bombing raids on Merseyside, while about 72,000 merchant and Royal Navy sailors were killed at sea. Around 75 per cent of the U-boats were destroyed, and 30,000 German sailors were killed.

Address 1-3 Rumford Street, Exchange Flags, Liverpool, L2 8SZ, +44 (0)151 227 2008, www.liverpoolwarmuseum.co.uk, info@westernapproaches.org.uk | Getting there Train to James Street or Moor Field | Hours Daily 10am–5pm | Tip Visit the Naval Memorial Waterfront, which commemorates British Merchant Navy casualties during World War II (Georges Pierhead, Liverpool, www.cwgc.org).

67 __ Witch Wood
A dead horse remembered

Lytham is a former shrimping port located where the River Ribble meets the Irish Sea. Lytham is famed for its white 1805 windmill, spacious coastal green, its high street of boutique shops, gentrified fisherman cottages, and upmarket eateries. It is often referred to as Lytham St Annes, reflecting its younger neighbour St Annes-on-the-Sea. Dating from the Bronze Age, the wider area is known as the Fylde Coast and includes the tourist resort of Blackpool.

Less well-known in Lytham is Witch Wood, a mile-long urban woodland steeped in local folklore. Often thought to be named after supernatural activity and evocative witches practicing sorcery deep in the forest, Witch Wood is actually named after something more mundane. The woodland runs alongside the railway line and was once part of the grounds of nearby Lytham Hall, the finest Georgian House in Lancashire.

The Clifton family, owners of Lytham Hall since 1606, held their ancestral seat at the hall, where a medieval Benedictine priory stood previously. John Talbot Clifton (1868–1928) used to enjoy riding horses throughout the estate. On 5 January, 1888, he suffered an accident whilst riding one of his favourite horses named The Witch, and the horse was killed and buried with a small gravestone simply inscribed 'The Witch, Died Jan 5th 1888'. The horse's burial spot is now within the wood named after it.

In 1963, with the Clifton family wealth squandered, the Guardian Royal Exchange took over Clifton Hall as its headquarters. Part of the derelict woodland was gifted to the Lytham St Annes Civic Society and opened in 1974 by the late Prince Philip as a community woodland. Witch Wood is a Site of Special Scientific Interest (SSSI), and all the trees are under preservation orders. The grave of 'The Witch' still rests amongst the woodland, but the sounds of haunted galloping are yet to be heard.

The Witch
Died Jan. 5th
1888

Address Bridge Road, Lytham St Annes, Lancashire, FY8 4EQ, www.visitlytham.info | Getting there Train to Lytham or Ansdell & Fairhaven | Hours Unrestricted | Tip Visit Layton Cemetery, burial place of Edwin Hughes ('Balaclava Ned' 1830–1927), the last survivor of the 1854 Charge of the Light Brigade during the Crimean War (Talbot Road, Blackpool, Lancashire).

68__ The Woodplumpton Witch

Buried beneath a boulder

In the Lancashire village of Woodplumpton, meaning 'plum tree farm', is the 12th century church of St Anne's (rebuilt in 1639 and 1900). Village stocks for punishing petty felons are just outside the church, as is a tall stone step for parishioners who travelled by horse.

Amongst the tombstones in St Anne's graveyard is a burial from 1705 that is said to have supernatural qualities. A large glacial boulder with a small plaque marks the spot where Meg Shelton has her final resting place. Meg (also known as Mag or Margery Hilton) was a woman who lived on the Fylde, a rural belt that stretches inland from the Fylde Coast. Meg was known as the 'Woodplumpton Witch' or 'Fylde Hag'. She is thought to have lived at Cuckoo Cottage between the villages of Singleton and Kirkham. Despite 100 years since the infamous 1612 Lancashire Witches at Pendle Hill, and with sorcery accusations dying out, Meg gained a reputation as a malevolent witch. She was blamed by local farmers for causing illness amongst their cattle or draining whole herds of their milk. Meg was also accused of 'shape-shifting' – the ability to take on the appearance of animals. She was indicted for summoning the Devil and casting satanic spells. In truth, she was probably a local 'wise woman', who practiced herbal remedies or helped deliver babies safely. Today, she might be classed somewhere between a pharmacist and a midwife.

Meg died from being crushed by a barrel. Accident or murder, no one quite knows, but, despite her reputation, she was laid to rest in consecrated ground. However, on two occasions, her corpse was seen near her grave after she apparently dug her way out. Meg was buried a third time, on this occasion head-first and a boulder placed on top to stop her 'escaping'. Today, strangers remember her 'deviant burial' by leaving flowers on her boulder grave.

Address St Anne's Church, Sandy Lane, Lower Bartle, Woodplumpton, Preston, PR4 0RX, www.stanneswoodplumpton.org.uk | Getting there Limited car parking available. Nearest Rail station is Preston, then a 15-minute taxi ride. This is a graveyard, so please respect its residents. | Hours Unrestricted | Tip Discover the dark heritage of witchcraft and medieval intrigue at Samlesbury Hall (Preston New Road, Samlesbury, Preston, www.samlesburyhall.co.uk).

69 Bletchley Park
Secret home to WWII codebreakers

Bletchley Park, also known as Station X, is an 1883 country house that became the principal centre of Allied codebreakers during World War II. In 1938, an ultra-secret Government Code and Cypher School was established here to decipher communications among the Axis Powers, most notably the German Enigma and Lorenz codes.

Nearly 10,000 people worked at Bletchley by 1945, three-quarters of them women who had middle-class backgrounds and degrees in languages, mathematics, physics or engineering. Winston Churchill described the staff as "the geese that laid the golden eggs and never cracked." It was not until 2009 that the British Government officially recognised the contributions of Bletchley Park.

The most notable codebreaker was Alan Turing who became the 'father' of computer science (see ch. 40). Turing led Hut 8 at Bletchley, the unit responsible for German naval cryptanalysis. Despite Turing's accomplishments, much of his work went unrecognised, as it was covered by the *Official Secrets Act*. Some of Turing's mathematical processes were not released to the UK National Archives until 2012 – such were their value to post-war cryptanalysis. Operations at Bletchley Park ceased in 1946, and all information about its activities was classified until the mid-1970s.

In 1993, Bletchley Park opened as a heritage attraction, and an independent National Museum of Computing opened in Block H on the park, well worth the separate admission charge. The park is a mixture of exhibitions and interactive displays with early computers, introductions to codebreaking and stories of wartime cyber-security.

Without breaking German codes, World War II may have continued for another two to four years with an uncertain outcome, but with the certain loss of even more lives. Estimates suggest 14 million or more people were saved because of the code breaking at Bletchley Park.

Address Bletchley Park, Sherwood Drive, Bletchley, Milton Keynes, MK3 6EB, +44 (0)190 864 0404, www.bletchleypark.org.uk, enquiries@bletchleypark.org.uk | **Getting there** Train to Bletchley, then walk southwest to Sherwood Drive | **Hours** See website for seasonal hours | **Tip** Bridego Bridge is the site of the 1963 Great Train Robbery, one of the biggest heists in English history (Rowden Lane, Leighton Buzzard, Ledburn).

70__ The D-Day Story
Tales from Operation Neptune

In the largest sea invasion in history, 156,000 Allied troops stormed five beaches along the Normandy coast on D-Day, 6 June, 1944 (see ch. 3). Around 50,000 German troops faced them. On that day alone, 4,414 Allied troops died, with 10,000 wounded or missing. Between 4,000–9,000 German troops were killed. As Colonel George Taylor stated on Omaha Beach, "Two kinds of people are staying on this beach – the dead and those who are going to die." Over 425,000 Allied and German troops died during the subsequent Battle of Normandy, and 20,000 French civilians were slain. The average age of the soldiers was 20 years.

The D-Day Story is the only museum in the UK dedicated to Operation Overlord, the Allied invasion of occupied Europe. With personal accounts of people who were there and brought to life through audio-visual presentations, alongside iconic artefacts, the story of D-Day is told. These are the stories of ordinary people working together to achieve the extraordinary.

The focus of D-Day Story is the liberation of Europe from Nazi Germany occupation. The story is told in three parts: Preparation, D-Day and Battle of Normandy and Legacy & The Overlord Embroidery. The embroidery, comprising 34 hand-stitched panels reaching 83 metres long, is the largest of its kind in the world. Commissioned by Lord Dulverton of Batsford (1915–92), it is a tribute to the sacrifice and heroism of D-Day. The D-Day Story also houses a restored LCT 7074, the last surviving landing craft tank.

Following a £5m transformation in 2018, the museum shifted its military focus to one that tells stories of people of that epic day. Other exhibits include Sherman and Churchill tanks, archive movies, maps, uniforms, and interactive displays. There are also reconstructions of the operations room at Southwick House, HQ of Allied forces, as well as a 1940s sitting room and Anderson bomb shelter.

Address Clarence Esplanade, Portsmouth, Hampshire, PO5 3NT, +44 (0)239 288 2555, www.theddaystory.com | Getting there Train to Portsmouth & Southsea, then a 20-minute walk | Hours See website for seasonal hours | Tip To learn about underwater warfare, pay a visit to the HMS *Alliance* Submarine Museum (Haslar Jetty Road, Gosport, Hampshire).

71 Diana's Burial Island
The People's Princess

On 31 August, 1997, the Mercedes-Benz sedan Diana, Princess of Wales had been travelling in crashed in the Pont de l'Alma tunnel in Paris. Lady Diana succumbed to her injuries. She was 36 years old. Her partner, Dodi Fayed, and driver, Henri Paul, were pronounced dead at the scene, though bodyguard Trevor Rees-Jones survived. A British inquest ruled Diana had been unlawfully killed, having been aggressively pursued by paparazzi and driven by an intoxicated chauffeur.

Diana – 'The People's Princess' – married Charles, Prince of Wales, in 1981. She grew up as Lady Diana, part of the aristocratic Spencer family, at the 500-year-old Althorp estate in Northamptonshire. The 13,000-acre estate is an example of British congenital entitlement, hereditary wealth, and social class division. Diana was the seventh cousin once removed to Prince Charles, and the couple had two children, William and Harry. With her husband and son heirs to the British throne, Diana was a popular yet controversial addition to the Royal Family. She craved media attention, yet she was also repulsed by it. Diana and Charles separated in 1992 and divorced in 1996. Charles had not forsaken his true love, Camilla Parker-Bowles, and Diana would famously reveal sordid realities about her marriage. Diana's death caused an unprecedented outpouring of public grief. The televised funeral at Westminster Abbey on 6 September was watched by an estimated 2.5 billion people across the globe.

Diana is buried at Althorp on a small island in the middle of an ornamental lake called the Oval. Diana's brother, Earl Charles Spencer, said the lake would 'act as a buffer against the interventions of the insane and ghoulish, the thick mud presenting a further line of defence.' While public access to the gravesite is strictly prohibited, visitors can visit a memorial close to the lake, as well as a nearby arboretum.

Address Located in Althorp Estate, Althorp, Northampton, NN7 4HG, +44 (0)160 477 0006, www.spencerofalthorp.com, info@althorp.com | Getting there Train to Northampton, then a 15-minute taxi ride | Hours See website for hours and ticket information | Tip Visit the Battlefield of Naseby 1665, a seminal conflict in English history and birthplace of the British Army (Naseby, Clipston Road, Northamptonshire, www.naseby.com).

72 International Bomber Command Centre

Controversial memorial to WWII bombing

The International Bomber Command Centre (IBCC) is a memorial and interpretive center around the World War II efforts of Allied Bomber Command. Opened in 2018, the IBCC tells the stories of those who suffered from and those who carried out the bombings.

Over a million men and women from 62 nations served or supported Bomber Command during World War II. Of the 125,000 aircrew, 72 per cent were killed, injured or taken as POWs, the highest attrition rate of any Allied unit. 57,871 men and women died whilst serving or supporting Bomber Command, and the average age at death was 23. Bomber Command was also involved in Operation Exodus – the repatriation of over 70,000 POWs from internment camps across Europe.

Strategic bombing during World War II is controversial and its effects still highly debated, as the Allies targeted industry and civilians, resulting in massive civilian casualties in German cities, including Hamburg and Dresden. Head of Bomber Command, Sir Arthur Harris – known as 'Bomber Harris' or 'Butcher Harris' – remains a provocative figure for his preference for area bombing and targeting the populace. The IBCC acts as a point of recognition, remembrance and reconciliation to help us understand the consequences.

The IBCC includes an education suite, interactive exhibitions in three galleries, visitor facilities, and a collections room. The IBCC also covers both war time and post-war reviews of the bombing campaigns, as well as impacts against enemy populations. A spire memorial, reflecting nearby Lincoln Cathedral and based upon the wingspan of a Lancaster bomber, is the only place in the world memorializing Bomber Command losses. Peace Gardens with geo-located trees for each of the 27 Lincolnshire bomber stations provide a sensory place for reflection.

Address Canwick Avenue, Lincoln, LN4 2HQ, +44 (0)152 251 4755, www.internationalbcc.co.uk, info@internationalbcc.co.uk | **Getting there** Train to Lincoln, then bus 1 to Rail Station Car Park | **Hours** See website for seasonal hours | **Tip** The Lincoln Tank Memorial is the world's first tank, built in Lincoln in 1915 (Brayford Way Roundabout, Ropewalk Tritton Road, Lincoln).

73 __Lincoln Castle & Jail

Kings and convicts, power and punishment

Built by William the Conqueror in 1068 on the site of a Roman for-tress, Lincoln Castle has dominated the local skyline for nearly one thousand years. The castle has witnessed numerous medieval battles, including the Battles of Lincoln in 1141 between King Stephen and Empress Matilda, and in 1217 between Henry III and Louis VIII of France during the First Barons' War. In 1215, King John and his nobles conceived the *Magna Carta*, a world-influencing charter that set rules and rights for liberty and society. One of four original cop-ies of the *Magna Carta* is held at the castle and can be viewed today. Henry VIII visited with Catherine Howard in 1541. The castle was besieged for the final time during the English Civil War in 1644, when Parliamentarian forces overwhelmed it. After a £22m restora-tion programme in 2015, the castle and jail offer visitors an immersive experience and a living history lesson.

From the 13th century onwards, the castle housed a prison, exe-cution site and burial ground. Convicts were hanged on the roof of Cobb Hall, while vast crowds watched the grisly spectacle. Lucy Tower became a burial ground, and the unconsecrated graves of exe-cuted prisoners still lie within. A red-brick Georgian gaol (jail) was built within the grounds in 1788 to imprison both felons and debtors, both men and women. During the 18th century, *gaols* were private businesses, and prisoners were forced to pay excessive fees for food and bedding.

In 1848, a new prison was designed to implement the 'separate system' – a pious regime intended to isolate prisoners from other inmates and corrupting influences. The prison chapel was constructed with individual standing pens, from which each convict could only see the vicar and no one else. The prison closed in 1878, though criminal trials in the Crown Court are still heard today, as the castle remains a seat of justice.

Address Lincoln Castle, Castle Square, Lincoln, Lincolnshire, LN1 3AA, +44 (0)152 255 4559, www.lincolncastle.com, lincoln_castle@lincolnshire.gov.uk | Getting there Train to Lincoln Central, and then a 17-minute walk | Hours See website for seasonal hours | Tip Explore the 'darker side' of Lincoln with ghostly (hi)stories on the Original Lincoln Ghost Walk (www.lincolnghostwalks.co.uk).

74 Rothwell Bone Crypt
Assemblage of our forgotten dead

In the former Viking settlement of Rothwell is Holy Trinity Church, home to a 700-year-old subterranean crypt containing the bones of 2,500 people. Dating from the 13th century and one of only two bone crypts in the country alongside St Leonards in Hythe, Kent (see ch. 99), the Rothwell Bone Crypt is a place of the entombed dead. Debunked theories of the bones' origins include Danes slain in Saxon warfare, soldiers killed at nearby Battles of Bosworth Field in 1485 or Nasebury in 1645, remains of monastic burials or mass victims of the Black Death.

Studies show that the crypt houses two radically different types of skulls. Type I skulls resemble medieval people, whilst Type II skulls are similar to those from the 17th century. Recent research by the University of Sheffield revealed that the bones included people from as late as 1900. Crypts, also known as charnel chapels or ossuaries, were a popular medieval religious structure found in all kinds of ecclesiastical complexes including parish churches, monasteries and even hospitals. They proliferated in England from the early 13th century until the Reformation in the mid-16th century, when they were banned.

The likely origin of the bones at Rothwell is from a gradual accumulation of churchyard burials when new graves were required. The bones would have been stacked in the crypt to make space for the newly deceased. Early Church doctrine, probably from Knights Templar beliefs, meant that only the femurs and skulls were needed for Resurrection and that God would be capable of finding the missing bones.

The Rothwell Crypt was rediscovered in the 1700s, allegedly by a clumsy gravedigger who fell through the doorway into a dark abyss and discovered himself in an awful assemblage of past generations. Today, the bones have been neatly organised and catalogued, and visitors can gaze at our forgotten dead.

Address Holy Trinity Church, Squires Hill, Rothwell, Kettering, Northamptonshire, NN14 6BQ, +44 (0)153 671 0268, www.rothwellholytrinity.org.uk/thebuilding | Getting there Train to Kettering, and then a 10-minute taxi ride | Hours Open most Sundays; call for schedule | Tip Rushton Triangular Lodge is a 1597 folly devoted to Catholicism and the Holy Trinity, built by Thomas Tresham – father of one of the 1605 Gunpowder Plotters (Desborough Road, Ruston, Kettering, NN14 1RP, www.english-heritage.org.uk).

75___Tyneham Ghost Village

The village that died for D-Day

Nestled in a secluded valley in the Purbeck Hills and close to the Jurassic Coast is the 'ghost village' of Tyneham. This rural idyll is not haunted by ghosts, but rather something truly real: state-sponsored abandonment and forced eviction. A village with evidence of Iron Age communities and Roman occupation, Tyneham was requisitioned by the War Office in 1943 and used for military training and artillery practice, specifically for the D-Day landings of occupied Europe in 1944 (see ch. 70).

The entire village and surrounding heathland were turned over to the military. The 225 residents were given a month's notice to leave the village with a promise they could return after the war. They never did. The last person to leave Tyneham posted a poignant note to the Army on the church door, 'Please treat the church and houses with care… We have given up our homes where many of us lived for generations to help win the war to keep men free. We shall return one day and thank you for treating the village kindly.'

In 1948, the Ministry of Defence placed a compulsory purchase order on the land, and it has remained an army range for live ammunition practice ever since. While many of the buildings are ruined by shelling, the church remains intact with an exhibition. Today, the village has become a kind of *heterotopia* – a disturbing space within a place, where time has been arrested and visitors are transported back to wartime England.

This solemn, tranquil village lost its villagers – or rather, they lost it. Whilst many of them campaigned to return to Tyneham, the Bond family, who had owned the majority of the village since 1683, were given compensation of £30,000 (£1.4m at present values). Yet the tenant villagers were only compensated for the value of the produce in their gardens. Some villagers did return, but only to be buried in the local village graveyard.

Address MOD Ranges, East Lulworth, Wareham, Dorset, BH20 5DE, +44 (0)192 940 4714, www.visit-dorset.com | **Getting there** Train to Wool | **Hours** Permitted access only; see website for hours | **Tip** Visit Imber and St Giles Church, another commandeered village used to demonstrate Spitfire and Hurricane airpower and now a military range (Warminster, www.imberchurch.org.uk/location.html).

76 Anaesthesia Heritage Centre

Passing gas is a life-affirming activity

Before advancements in pain relief, dying was an excruciating affair. In medieval times, people often led brutish lives followed by an agonizing death. In those days, death was seen to 'tame' life and offer salvation into a better afterlife. While herbal pain relief had been around since antiquity, the science of anaesthesia is a 19th century discovery. The Anaesthesia Heritage Centre tells compelling tales of pioneering scientists, whose efforts enabled lifesaving surgery of the modern era.

In 1800, Humphry Davy noted that nitrous oxide "appears capable of destroying physical pain, and may probably be used with great advantage during surgical operations". By 1824, Henry Hill Hickman was using carbon dioxide to operate on animals, establishing the principles of inhalation anaesthesia. In 1846, William Morton first successfully used diethyl ether as a general anaesthetic, followed shortly after by the first effective use of anaesthesia in the UK at University College Hospital, London. The year after saw the introduction of chloroform, while in 1848 the first recorded fatality from chloroform was recorded: Hannah Greener, aged 15.

Despite the dangers, John Snow gave chloroform to Queen Victoria during her childbirth to Prince Leopold in 1853. By 1908, anaesthetics came under the auspices of the Royal Society of Medicine. The horror of World War I provided fertile ground for the development of anaesthesia, and it has developed ever since to help provide life affirming surgery today.

The Anaesthesia Heritage Centre is testament to those anaesthetists and presents oral histories of their deeds. The Centre is also home to a bizarre collection of devices used to administer what is one of the greatest discoveries in medical history.

Address 21 Portland Place, London, W1B 1PY, +44 (0)207 631 1650 + option 7, www.anaesthetists.org/Home/Heritage-centre, heritage@anaesthetists.org | Getting there Tube to Regent's Park (Bakerloo Line) | Hours Mon–Fri 10am–4pm | Tip At the British Dental Museum, be prepared to discover painful dental practices of the past (64 Wimpole Street, London, www.bda.org/museum).

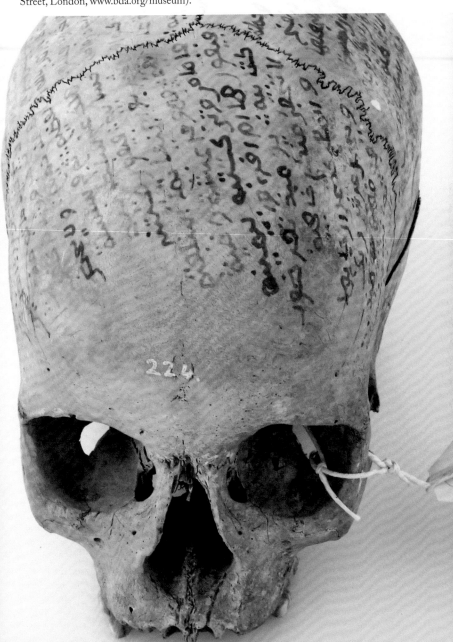

*77*__Animals in War Memorial

Remembering animals who died during conflict

The Animals in War Memorial commemorate creatures killed in vast numbers through agonising deaths during wartime. During World War I, eight million horses and countless mules died, transporting troops and munitions in the midst of shellfire. Dogs' innate qualities of intelligence and devotion served the military master well, as faithful hounds ran messages, detected mines, or dug out casualties. Over 300,000 pigeons, often wounded, flew vital messages over long distances when communication was all but impossible. Other animals chosen for their natural instincts included elephants, camels, oxen, cats, canaries and even glow worms.

One of the animals who served during the conflict was Rob, a collie (War Dog No. 471/332 SAS), who was awarded the PDSA Dickin Medal on 22 January, 1945. During his canine service, Rob took part in North African landings with an infantry unit. He later served with the Special Air Service in Italy as a SAS patrol dog, lying-up behind enemy lines. Rob's presence with his human combatants saved many of them from discovery and subsequent capture. He made over 20 parachute descents.

Unveiled in 2004 and constructed in Portland stone and bronze, the 58-foot-wide monument has two different levels and a dominating wall between them. The imagery invites visitors into the monument to become personally informed. On the lower level, two heavily laden bronze mules struggle through an arena, symbolising war experiences, as they approach a flight of steps that lead through the wall. Beyond the wall, on the upper level, a bronze horse and dog bear witness to the loss of their comrades and also signify hope for the future. On the outside of the wall, ghostly silhouettes are carved to represent animals lost in conflict, including Rob the War Dog. They had no choice but to serve, and this monument is a powerful tribute to their sacrifices.

Address Park Lane, London, W1K 7QF, www.animalsinwar.org.uk | Getting there Tube to Marble Arch (Central Line), then walk to Brook Gate in Hyde Park | Hours Unrestricted | Tip Visit the nearby hidden pet cemetery behind Victoria Gate Lodge (adjoining Bayswater Road, Hyde Park).

78__Barts Pathology Museum
Glimpse into our bodies and souls

Barts Pathology Museum is based in St Bartholomew's Hospital and houses over 5,000 medical specimens built up over two centuries. Spanning three mezzanine levels, the museum is a part of Queen Mary University of London. It has been named by CNN as one of the 'Top 10 Weirdest Museums in the World'. However, there is nothing weird about bringing pathology alive, and the museum does so with quirky and interesting events. It is a modern dynamic venue as well as a medical humanities hub for critical connoisseurs and cultural insiders.

St Barts is a teaching hospital founded in 1123 by Rahere, an Anglo-Norman monk. It was refounded by Henry VIII after the Dissolution of the Monasteries. Barts Pathology Museum was founded by pathologist James Paget, best recognised for identifying a bone malady known as Paget's Disease, and opened in 1879 by the future King Edward VII. Author Sir Arthur Conan Doyle chose the museum as the site for the first fortuitous meeting of his sleuth Sherlock Holmes and his companion Dr Watson. The museum is also home to the skull of John Bellingham, the assassin of Prime Minister Spencer Perceval in 1812 (see ch. 96). He was sentenced to be 'hanged and anatomized', the latter being an extra punishment after death.

Other museum exhibits include deformed and diseased body parts, a gout swollen hand and an inguinal hernia dating from 1750. Skeletons of conjoined twins and a liver dented by years of wearing tight corsets are displayed alongside a brain perforated during a frontal lobotomy, a dissected rat that died of tuberculosis and cervical vertebra from convicts of judicial hangings. The museum abides by regulations set out by the UK Human Tissue Authority to showcase humanity in all its fragility. The medical specimens, far from being weird or macabre, are glimpses of our mortal bodies and, ultimately, insight into our souls.

Address Robin Brook Centre, 3rd Floor, St Bartholomew's Hospital, West Smithfield, London, EC1A 7BE, +44 (0)207 882 5555, www.qmul.ac.uk/pathologymuseum | **Getting there** Tube to Barbican (Hammersmith & City, Circle and Metropolitan Lines) | **Hours** By appointment only | **Tip** Sir William Wallace was a Scottish Knight known as 'Braveheart' who was hung, drawn, and quartered in Smithfield in 1305. Visit his memorial at The Elms in Smithfield (57A West Smithfield, London, EC1A 9DS).

79 Battle of Britain Memorial

Remembering the 'Few'

After France surrendered in 1940, Britain expected an invasion by Nazi Germany. As Hitler planned the offensive against Great Britain, Operation Sea Lion, the first major military campaign fought entirely by air forces, began. The Battle of Britain raged in the skies above the English Channel and southeast England from 10 July to 31 October, 1940 (see ch. 66). The Royal Air Force (RAF) and Fleet Air Arm of the Royal Navy defended Britain with only 640 aircraft from relentless attacks by the German Luftwaffe and their 2,600-strong fleet. British Prime Minister Winston Churchill made a rousing parliamentary speech on 20 August, 1940. He stated, 'Never in the field of human conflict was so much owed by so many to so few.'

The Battle of Britain Memorial is a collection of monuments and interactive displays that give a sense of contemplation and gratitude to those who fought and died. The average age of pilots in the battle, including those from Poland, Ireland, Canada, and (former) Czechoslovakia, was 20 years old, and they were paid a salary of £264. But the life expectancy during the battle period was just four weeks, and 544 Allied pilots were killed. The German name for the Battle is *Luftschlacht um England*, or Air Battle for England, in which over 2,500 German pilots also lost their lives.

Alluding to Shakespeare's famous quote in *Henry V*, 'We few, we happy few, we band of brothers,' the 'few' were 2,936 airmen of RAF Fighter Command. The Battle of Britain was a turning point in World War II, as Britain emerged victorious, having halted Nazi plans for British subjugation. Allied pilots with five 'kills' or more were hailed as 'Aces,' and the planes used in the fighting, such as the Spitfire and the Hurricane, became immortalised. The Battle of Britain encapsulated heroism and sacrifice, but the toll was the deaths of many young men, both British and German.

Address New Dover Road, Folkestone, Kent, CT18 7JJ, +44 (0)130 324 9292, www.battleofbritainmemorial.org, enquiries@battleofbritainmemorial.org | Getting there Train to Folkestone Central, then bus 102 Dover to Alexandra Road | Hours See website for seasonal hours | Tip Make your way down the ZigZag Path, a winding cave grotto walkway built to provide employment for World War I veterans (The Leas, Lower Sandgate Road, Folkestone, Kent, CT20 2EB).

80 __ Bethlem: Museum of the Mind

'Pray remember the poor lunatics' at Bedlam Asylum

Founded in 1247, Bethlem Royal Hospital was an infamous mental asylum synonymous with chaos and cruelty. Referred to as 'Bedlam', the psychiatric institution now exhibits archives and art that chart the difficulties of mental healthcare. Patients whose work is on display includes Richard Dadd, noted for his detailed fairy paintings. He was locked up after he murdered his father.

While the hospital has moved locations across London during its history, from the 17th to 19th centuries, the brutal ill-treatment meted out to patients became a fee-paying spectator event. Ruthless beatings of patients in the original Bedlam were regarded as a therapeutic shock for the mentally ill. This voyeurism of violence enticed Georgian and Victorian elites to visit the 'looney bin' as a social occasion. However, asylum tourism gave way to moral management, and reforms in mental healthcare were gradually made. *The Lunacy Act 1845* stopped the practice of visiting asylums. Yet old-world asylums still loom large in our cultural imagination as places of fear and malpractice. Popular culture proliferates this dread, with Bedlam often used as a backdrop for tales of horror and the supernatural.

But despite cultural anxieties of asylums, the value of these early mental institutions became a foundation for the modern study of the mind. Today, Bethlem: Museum of the Mind goes beyond Bedlam. One patient, Barrington, depicts in her painting the hospital and its grounds full of happy people. She suggests, "I think it's important not to try and draw a veil or conceal anything about our long and sometimes difficult history, but it's important to show there is hope too." Asylum tourism may still exist today at Bedlam, but the focus today is art and patients' resilience and recovery.

Address Bethlem Royal Hospital, Monks Orchard Road, Beckenham, Kent, BR3 3BX, +44 (0)203 228 4227, www.museumofthemind.org.uk | **Getting there** Train to West Wickham, then walk 15 minutes | **Hours** Wed–Fri 10am–5pm, Mon & Tue pre-booked tours only | **Tip** You can also visit the Imperial War Museum where Bedlam was located from 1815 to 1930 (Lambeth Road, London, www.iwm.org.uk).

81 Clink Prison Museum

Tales of torment and torture

Built on the site of one of England's oldest and most notorious medieval prisons is the Clink Prison Museum. The Clink Prison dates back to 1144, and with tales of torment and torture, the museum blends serious history with schlocky horror, or 'edutainment'. However, the museum is also a research centre for the study of crime and penal heritage, as well as social and religious practices from yesteryear. Positioned in the heart of Southwark and considered more wicked than its neighbouring City of London, the Clink was home to various sinners spanning 600 years.

The Clink's walls held many significant figures, including John Rogers, the man responsible for translating the Bible into English from Latin during the reign of Queen 'Bloody' Mary I, whom the Queen sentenced to be burned at the stake for heresy in 1555. Royalist supporters were imprisoned here during the English Civil War (1642–1651), as were numerous Puritans, including Henry Barrowe and John Greenwood in 1593, who were later hanged at Tyburn. The congregation of their English Separatist Church, known as the Pilgrim Fathers, sailed to America on the Mayflower in 1620. In 1780, the Gordon Riots, motivated by anti-Catholic sentiment, saw the Clink destroyed, and it was never rebuilt.

The Clink Prison Museum presents the scandals of old London through hands-on experiences, artefacts and interactive exhibitions. Tales of torment and the misfortunes of inmates of the infamous Clink Prison are retold in the museum. Visitors will learn that the term 'The Clink', which is still used today, most likely acquired its name from the sound of the iron shackles as they were hammered closed around the wrists and ankles of each prisoner. Today, visitors can immerse themselves in a bygone age – and even go on a ghost hunt through the prison at night – where penal justice was brutal and unforgiving.

Address 1 Clink Street, London, SE1 9DG, +44 (0)207 403 0900, www.clink.co.uk | Getting there Tube to London Bridge (Jubilee and Northern Lines) | Hours Daily 10am – 6pm | Tip Southwark Cathedral, London's oldest cathedral, is the site of medieval heresy trials and the tomb of Edmund Shakespeare, brother of William Shakespeare (London Bridge, London, SE1 9DA, www.cathedral.southwark.anglican.org).

82 Cross Bones Graveyard

R.I.P 'The Outcast Dead'

A short distance from Shakespeare's Globe Theatre is Cross Bones Graveyard, a medieval burial site holding the mortal remains of an estimated 15,000 paupers. The cemetery closed in 1853 on grounds that it was completely overcharged with the dead. More than half of the deceased were children.

For centuries, the site was an unconsecrated, mass burial pit for one of London's poorest and most violent suburbs, formerly known as The Mint. It is believed that Cross Bones is the final resting place for the Winchester Geese – medieval prostitutes licenced by the Bishop of Winchester to work in the brothels of The Liberty of the Clink, which lay outside the law of the City of London. Denied a Christian burial, the Winchester Geese gained their derisive name, perhaps, after the custom of baring their white bosoms to entice customers. To be 'bitten by a Winchester Goose' was to contract a sexually transmitted disease.

Rediscovered in the 1990s, Cross Bones is now a community initiative to commemorate London's 'outcast dead'. Today, the site is unofficially memorialised by an array of mementos and other artwork, as well as flowers and plants. A campaign for a permanent memorial garden is currently underway, and the site has become a focus for the way the Church treats women.

Cross Bones has also taken on supernatural and spiritualist themes. At Halloween, rituals at the graveyard provide for ceremonial mediumship and urban shamanism. Resident poet and graveyard campaigner John Constable even suggests that a spirit of a medieval prostitute has visited him. He calls her 'The Goose', and she led him to the burial site. He claims that the ghost dictated a poem to him: *For tonight in Hell / They are tolling the bell / For the Whore that lay at the Tabard, / And well we know / How the carrion crow / Doth feast in our Cross Bones Graveyard.*

Address 18-22 Redcross Way, Camberwell, London, SE1 1SD, +44 (0)207 403 3393, www.crossbones.org.uk, info@bost.org.uk | Getting there Tube to Borough (Northern Line) | Hours Unrestricted | Tip Vigils to the outcast dead have been held at Cross Bones since 2004. Gather at the gates at 6.45pm on the 23rd of every month.

83 David Bowie Mural

'Major Tom' is dead

The iconic singer, musician and art collector David Robert Jones, better known as David Bowie, has been called 'rock's greatest self-inventor'. As one of the most influential musicians of the 20th century, he left a musical and artistic legacy of creativity, reinvention and visual presentation. With over 100 million albums sold worldwide, Bowie became one of the top musical artists of all time. He died of liver cancer at the age of 69 on 10 January, 2016, and he was featured on the *Forbes* 2017 list of top-earning deceased celebrities, with an estimated posthumous income of £8.5m.

On a wall of Morley's department store, opposite Brixton tube station in London, is a large, graffiti-style mural of David Bowie. Painted by artist James Cochran in 2013, the portrait is of Bowie dressed as his alter-ego Ziggy Stardust as he appeared on the cover of his 1973 album *Aladdin Sane*. Cohran's mural has since become an unofficial memorial shrine to the cultural artiste, as thousands of Bowie fans have left notes and flowers there, and even written commemorative messages on the wall.

Bowie suggested that the vibrant lightning bolt across Stardust's face represented duality of mind, and it remains a popular cultural icon today. Bowie was born near the mural at 40 Stansfield Road. Brixton also has its own local currency – the Brixton Pound – and Bowie is featured on the B£10.

In 1985, Bowie's schizophrenic half-brother, Terry Burns, committed suicide by jumping onto a railway track, inspiring Bowie's 1993 song *Jump They Say*. Bowie's final album, *Blackstar*, is loaded with mortality symbolism. The title track suggests a light flickering out, while the artwork fades away when exposed to light. The music video features a 'Major Tom' skeleton inside a spacesuit – a reference to his 1969 song 'Space Oddity'. Bowie's ashes are scattered in Indonesia, according to his Buddhist beliefs.

Address 472-488 Brixton Road, London, SW9 8BN | Getting there Tube to Brixton (Victoria Line) | Hours Unrestricted | Tip There is a grave of an unknown London girl, buried in Roman times, that was found in 1995 when the Gherkin was being built. She was reburied there after construction was finished (30 St Mary Axe, London, EC3A 8BF).

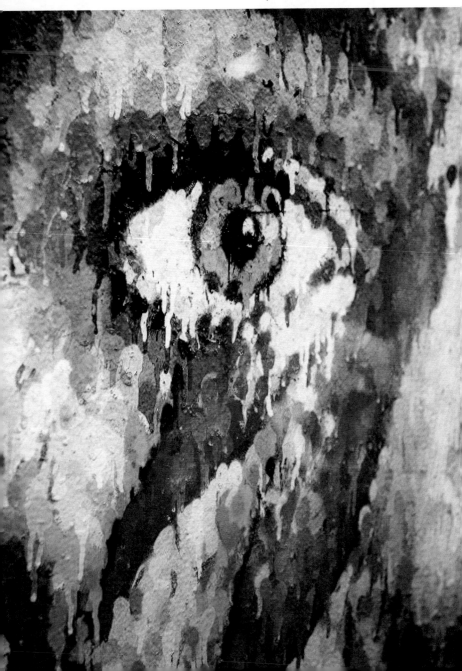

84 Execution Dock

Pirates hanged to the 'Marshal's Dance'

For over 400 years, Execution Dock was used to hang pirates, smugglers and mutineers who had been sentenced to death by the Admiralty Courts. The Admiralty's legal jurisdiction was for all crimes committed at sea, and the dock was symbolically located just beyond the low tide mark in the River Thames. Now long gone, the dock consisted of a scaffold for hanging. Convicts were brought from Marshalsea or Newgate prison and paraded across London Bridge and past the Tower of London. As was customary for prisoners sentenced to death, they were offered a quart of ale at a local pub on the way to the gallows.

Spectators often lined the banks of the River Thames to get a good view of the executions. A particular cruelty was reserved for pirates, who were hanged with a shortened rope, resulting in an excruciatingly slow death from strangulation. This practice was nicknamed the 'Marshal's Dance' because limbs would continue to 'dance' during asphyxiation. Bodies were often left hanging until three tides had washed over them.

Corpses were also tarred and placed in gibbets (cages) along the river as warnings to other bandits. Captain William Kidd, the infamous Scottish pirate, met his end at Execution Dock in 1701 at the age of 47. After being hanged twice, his corpse was gibbeted and left in the Thames estuary for three years.

While the actual location of Execution Dock is disputed, the last execution there in 1830 was of George Davis and William Watts for piracy in the Cyprus mutiny. Current contenders for the location are the Sun Warf building, The Prospect of Whitby pub, the Captain Kidd pub and, likeliest location – the Town of Ramsgate pub. Look for a small passageway behind the Ramsgate pub that leads to Wapping Old Stairs. Descend the stairs at low tide, watching out for mud and moss, and you'll be on the river bank where many executions took place.

Address 62 Wapping Street, London, E1W 2PN | Getting there Tube to Tower Hill (Circle and District Lines) | Hours Unrestricted | Tip The Prospect of Whitby pub was the hostelry of choice for 17th century 'Hanging' Judge Jeffreys. Stop in for a pint and a gander at its replica gallows (57 Wapping Street, London).

85 The Flask Public House

Serving fresh corpses for early autopsies

Most historic pubs in England have grisly pasts, and The Flask is no exception. Harking back to the day when Highgate was a village on the outskirts of London, the oldest part of the pub dates back to 1663. Past patrons include highwayman Dick Turpin (see ch. 23), satirist William Hogarth, philosopher Karl Marx, and literary icons Byron, Shelley, Keats and opium enthusiast Coleridge.

The Flask is apparently one of London's most ghostly pubs. Apparitions reported include a Spanish barmaid from the 1800s, who hanged herself in the cellar because of her unrequited love for the married publican. Another supposed phantom is a cavalier soldier, who seemingly appears and then vanishes through a pillar in the middle of the lounge.

In addition to the alleged paranormal activity, the pub was actually home to some of the first-ever autopsies. As the Enlightenment gave way to increased medical advancements, anatomy became established as a field of study and required fresh cadavers. Fortunately, the *Murder Act 1751* (repealed in 1973), exacted further punishment on executed murderers, stating, 'No murderer be buried but their corpse used for public dissection.'

But, with capital punishment on the wane during the 19th century, and before the *Anatomy Act 1832*, the supply of corpses for anatomy studies became scarce. The solution, at the time, was for illegal body-snatching of the freshly buried dead. It became a pervasive and lucrative trade, with increasing demand for corpses from anatomists and medical schools. It remains unclear why autopsies were carried out at The Flask, but in the early 19th century, body-snatchers – known as resurrectionists – would bring stolen, fresh corpses from nearby Highgate Cemetery for dissection. Secretly performed in what is now the Committee Room, autopsies explored the world of human anatomy and, ultimately, informed medical science.

Address Highgate, 77 Highgate West Hill, Highgate, London, N6 6BU, +44 (0)208 348 7346, www.theflaskhighgate.com, flask@fullers.co.uk | Getting there Tube to Highgate (Northern Line) | Hours Mon–Sat noon–11pm, Sun noon–10.30pm | Tip Enjoy classic pub fare at Spaniards Inn, where Dick Turpin's father was once the landlord (Spaniards Road, Hampstead, London, www.thespaniardshampstead.co.uk).

86 Highgate Cemetery

Sightseeing in the mansions of the dead

Romantic decay and graves of illustrious figures make Highgate Cemetery an important funerary landscape. Designed by Stephen Geary in 1839, Highgate is one of London's 'Magnificent Seven' cemeteries. Highgate helped alleviate the unsanitary overcrowding of burial grounds. Built in the Victorian Gothic Revival imagination, the cemetery doubled in size by 1854 with the addition of East Highgate. Highgate remains open to new burials, with over 170,000 people buried in around 53,000 graves.

Highgate is notable for its *de facto* status as a nature reserve, where visitors can sightsee in the mansions of the dead. Imposing tombstones, architectural catacombs and ostentatious graves litter the eerily and overgrown scenery. Once used as a location for the *Hammer House of Horror* film series, Highgate became popular with Gothic tales of body-snatching, desecration and vampires.

The cemetery is home to some famous dead. Most notable is Karl Marx, father of Communism, whose tomb, ironically, attracts a fee to visit, as it is on private property! Other notable residents include novelist George Eliot, writer Douglas Adams, poet Christina Rossetti, impresario Malcolm McLaren and pop artist Patrick Caulfield. Television presenter Jeremy Beadle is also interned at Highgate, as is the singer George Michael, who is buried in an unmarked grave. Adam Worth, a famous criminal and possible inspiration for Sherlock Holmes's nemesis, Professor Moriarty, is also an eternal guest of Highgate.

As cremation has become the prevalent way of disposing the dead, many graves at Highgate reflect cultural changes and social upheavals. Yet, with over 100,000 visitors to Highgate every year, the dead are not left in peace. Instead, the resting place of our dead has become a backdrop for leisure outings and objects of the tourist gaze. 'Death tourism' has arrived back into the public consciousness.

Address Highgate Cemetery, Swain's Lane, Highgate, London, N6 6PJ, +44 (0)208 340 1834, www.highgatecemetery.org | **Getting there** Tube to Archway (Northern Line) | **Hours** See website for seasonal hours | **Tip** The oldest 'park cemetery' in London is Kensal Green Catacombs (Harrow Road, London, www.kensalgreencemetery.com).

87__Ilford Pet Cemetery

A mortuary gem for beloved animals

Ilford Pet Cemetery is nestled behind an animal hospital and through a wooden archway inscribed, 'They Are Ever In Our Thoughts, Love Never Dies'. Founded in 1928 by the People's Dispensary for Sick Animals (PDSA) and hosting over 3,000 animal burials, the cemetery closed in the 1960s. After years of neglect, it reopened in 2007 with funding from the National Lottery. The opening ceremony included a rendition of *The Last Post* and a homing pigeon fly-past (though they scattered on hearing loud noises).

Ilford Pet Cemetery includes the graves of 12 Dickin Medal winners, a military recognition for animal heroism in the face of conflict. Equivalent to the human award of the Victoria Cross, a fifth of all Dickin awards are buried at Ilford. Awardees include Mary of Exeter, a pigeon that was injured on each of the four flights she made carrying messages from wartime France. With a shrapnel wound in her neck, her owner made Mary a collar brace that kept her head up, and she lived another ten years.

Simon the Able Seacat is the only cat to be awarded the Dickin Medal. Trapped aboard HMS *Amethyst* by Chinese communist rebels on the Yangtze River in 1949, Simon survived after being blown up with the captain, who died. His fame grew, and Simon was brought back to Britain, which proved to be the death of him. He caught cat flu and died while in quarantine.

While most of the dead are canines and felines, there are also budgies, horses, and rabbits. There is even a monkey called Ginner, who distinguished himself during the war by warning his deaf master of the approach of incoming bombs.

At the onset of World War II, frightened pet owners had their animals put down for fear of their falling into enemy hands. The PDSA destroyed up to 750,000 animals in the first week of the war. This tragedy was referred to as the 'September holocaust'.

Address 495 High Road, Ilford, London, IG1 1TX | Getting there Train to Seven Kings | Hours Unrestricted | Tip Visit the World Trade Centre artwork, a steel sculpture by artist Mia Ando in Queen Elizabeth Olympic Park, honouring the 67 Britons who died in New York on 11 September, 2001 (near the Aquatic Center, Carpenters Road, London, www.since911.com/wtc-artwork-911).

88__Jack the Ripper Museum

Forget the villain, remember the victims

Jack the Ripper was a serial killer, who was never caught and remains one of the world's most infamous criminals. The Ripper terrified London from 7 August till 10 September, 1888 (see ch. 101), murdering and mutilating numerous women, including those victims known as the Canonical Five. The murderer may have had a knowledge of anatomy – and an acute case of misogyny.

Jack the Ripper Museum opened in 2015 to much controversy. It recreates the East End of London, where the murders took place. Originally planned as a Museum of Women's History, the focus changed to a more tabloid interpretation of events. The five-room exhibition includes a mocked-up morgue, the bedroom of one of the victims and a murder scene with an effigy of PC Watkins standing over the corpse.

Violence against 'ladies of the night' in Victorian Britain was tolerated, even accepted. Jack the Ripper has captured popular imagination with the mystery of the villain rather than the memory of the victims. But the women themselves deserve to be recognized for who they were during their lives.

The first victim was Mary Ann Nichols (43), christened in 1851. She married William Nichols in 1864 and struggled with alcoholism. Annie Chapman (47), the second victim, had three children. She had a son with disabilities, and her daughter died aged 12. The third victim was Elisabeth Stride (44), a Swedish immigrant who operated a coffee shop with her husband John until 1875. Catherine Eddowes (46) was the fourth victim. She became an orphan in 1857 and fell on hard times after having three children. The final victim was Mary Jane Kelly (25). Aged 16, she married a coal miner, who later died in an accident and left her to live in poverty. Her body was extensively mutilated. Ultimately, the victims were women who fell through the net of Victorian society, and the villain was a cruel sociopath.

Address 12 Cable Street, Aldgate, London, E1 8JG +44 (0)207 488 9811, www.jacktherippermuseum.com | **Getting there** Tube to Aldgate East (District and Hammersmith & City Lines) | **Hours** Fri–Sun 10am–5.30pm | **Tip** Visit the Golden Boy of Pye Corner, the gold figure of a child, on the site where the 1666 Great Fire of London eventually burnt out (Cock Lane & Giltspur Street, London).

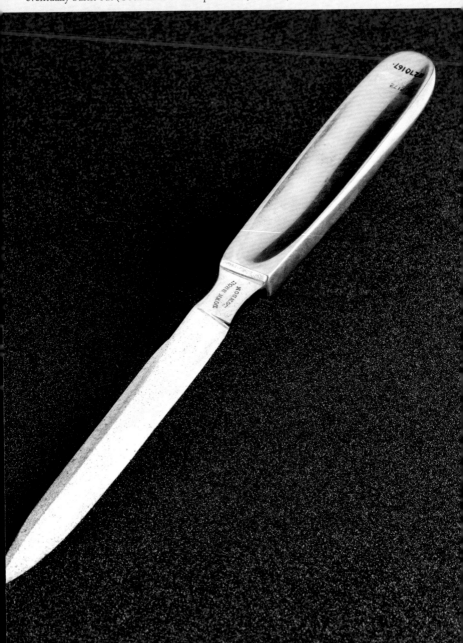

89 Kelvedon Hatch

The nuclear bunker below

About thirty miles east of London is Kelvedon Hatch – a large 'secret' bunker built to house the government in the event of nuclear war. One of 18 nuclear bunkers across the UK, Kelvedon Hatch, with three levels at 35,000-square-feet and 125 feet underground, offers visitors a terrifying glimpse into post-apocalyptic life. Built on land requisitioned from local farmer J.A. Parish in 1952 at a cost of £1.5 million, the site served the ROTOR programme as part of Britain's air defence. The bunker was a hardened Sector Operations Centre (SOC) for RAF Fighter Command. From the 1960s to late 1980s, in the event of a nuclear strike, the site would have been the Regional Government Headquarters (RGHQ), tasked with population survival.

Accommodating up to 600 personnel, the entrance to the bunker is through an inconspicuous brick bungalow set amongst the trees. Inside the façade of the bungalow, which would have been heavily guarded, a 91-metre tunnel leads to the underground chambers. Furnished with equipment that was state-of-the-art at the time, the bunker has air conditioning, heating, its own water supply, and an array of telecommunications and military systems. The bunker also has sleeping quarters, a canteen and kitchen, a BBC studio and a medical bay, as well as a mortuary with a collection of coffins. In 2010, the British survival horror movie *S.N.U.B* – acronym for Secret Nuclear Underground Bunker – was filmed here.

Decommissioned by the Government in 1992, after refurbishing costs of over £10 million, the bunker was sold to the original Parish family. Today, the visitor experience is a surreal reminder of Armageddon, as nuclear tourism goes on beneath the Essex countryside. The private museum has not been over-curated and is, perhaps, more authentic for its random artefacts and its chaotic and arbitrary displays, each adding to a sense of apocalypse.

Address Kelvedon Hatch, Brentwood, Essex, CM15 0LA, +44 (0)127 736 4883, www.secretnuclearbunker.com | Getting there Train to Brentwood or Shenfield, then a 15-minute taxi ride | Hours See website for seasonal hours | Tip At the Essex Witch Hunt Victims Memorial, you will discover Britain's greatest hysteria in the 16th and 17th centuries (Castle Park Gardens, High Street, Colchester, Essex).

90 London Necropolis Railway

A train to transport the dead

Cemeteries in London before the *Burial Act 1852* were literally over-flowing, and effluvium from decaying corpses polluted water supplies. Bodies were dug from graves and cremated to make burial space for the newly deceased. The London Necropolis and National Mauso-leum Company took one initiative to tackle this crisis in 1852, when they developed Brookfield Cemetery in Surrey, the UK's largest burial site. However, the cemetery was 23 miles from London, too far for a horse-drawn hearse. The London Necropolis Railway was built to transport the dead to their final resting place.

The railway opened in 1854 between Waterloo Bridge Station and Brookwood Cemetery. It had private rooms for funerals, a chapel, and a hydraulic lift to raise and lower coffins. Existing railway arches were used as mortuaries. The route was chosen for the beautiful scenery that would comfort mourners on the train. With 2,000 bodies a day transported at its peak, the Necropolis Railway carried both mourners and the deceased, though only one party had a return ticket.

In 1902, the terminus was demolished, and a new building opened at Westminster Bridge Road. The grand, red-brick frontage was designed by Cyril Bazett Tubbs and intended to be as un-funereal as possible. The new station also had separate areas for the social classes. Even the dead travelled according to their social status in life.

When the train arrived at Brookfield, cortèges alighted either at South Station (for Anglican burials) or North Station (for Non-Conformists). Wakes were held at the stations afterwards, and bars served snacks and pints. But in 1909, the introduction of the motor hearse made the railway redundant. The London Necropolis Railway was destroyed during the Blitz in 1941. Today, only the elegant façade of the station remains.

Address 121 Westminster Bridge Road, London, SE1 7HR | Getting there Tube to Lambeth North (Bakerloo Line) | Hours Unrestricted | Tip Visit the tomb of Captain Bligh, the infamous Captain of the HMS *Bounty* mutinied in 1791. His grave lies in what is now the Garden Museum (5 Lambeth Palace Road, London, www.gardenmuseum.org.uk).

91 Lord Lucan's House
A disappeared aristocrat wanted for murder

Lord Richard John Bingham, the 7th Earl of Lucan, was a debonair, Anglo-Irish aristocrat, who vanished after being suspected of murder. Born in 1934, Lucan attended Eton College and then joined the Coldstream Guards. Lucan developed a gambling habit and earned himself the nickname Lucky. Known for expensive tastes, he was once considered for the role of James Bond. Despite his losses often exceeding his winnings, Lucan left his merchant banker job and became a professional gambler.

In 1963, he married Veronica Duncan and had three children. But the marriage collapsed in 1972 from mounting debts and accusations of his domestic abuse. Lucan moved out of the Belgravia family home, and a bitter divorce battle ensued. On 7 November, 1974, the family's nanny Sandra Rivett, aged 29, was found bludgeoned to death from a blunt weapon in the basement of 46 Lower Belgrave Street. Her body was dumped into a mail bag. Lady Lucan was also attacked and beaten, but she managed to escape to the Plumbers Arms pub. She shouted, 'Murder, murder… I think my neck has been broken. He's tried to kill me!' She identified the assailant as her 39-year-old husband. Meanwhile, Lucan drove to a friend's mansion in Uckfield. He later left the property and was never ever seen again. Blood stains and a piece of metal pipe were later found in his car at the port of Newhaven.

Some accounts suggest Lucan killed Rivett by mistake, the true target being his wife. Hundreds of unsubstantiated sightings of Lucan have since been reported. Rumours of his demise include his suicide, being murdered himself, or living in Africa and then being eaten by a tiger. Lucan was declared legally dead in 1999. In 2016, a death certificate was issued allowing his son to inherit the Lucan Earldom. In 2017, Lady Lucan was found dead at the same house, having committed suicide at the age of 80.

Address 46 Lower Belgrave Street, Belgravia, London, SW1W 0LN | Getting there Tube to London Victoria (Circle, District and Victoria Lines) | Hours Unrestricted from the outside only | Tip Walk past the Embassy of Iran, where the Iranian Embassy siege and SAS raid took place in 1980 (16 Princes Gate, South Kensington, London).

92 The Maidstone Mummy

A mummified memento mori

The star of Maidstone Museum is undoubtedly a well-preserved, if not haunting, mummified Egyptian corpse. The female mummy, called Ta-Kesh for 150 years but now named Ta-Kush (meaning 'Kushite lady, daughter of Osiris') is 2,700 years old. Ta-Kush was originally thought to be 14 years old, but research in 2016 suggests she is in her mid-20s. She was brought to England in the 1820s and studied by Samuel Birch of the British Museum and local doctor Hugh Welch Diamond. Ta-Kush was given to Dr Diamond's cousin, Mr Charles, whose collections formed the Charles Museum, which later became the Maidstone Museum.

Derived from the Latin term *mumia* (meaning embalmed corpse), mummification was a defining custom of ancient Egyptian society, preserving the body to ensure a safe passage to the afterlife. Imbued with deep religious significance, mummification was also practiced by other ancient cultures, including the Chinese, the Guanches of the Canary Islands, and many Inca communities of South America. The blackened corporeal face of Ta-Kush is a *memento mori*, a reminder of our own mortality. For many people, mummies evoke a sinister sense of the macabre, conjuring up popular images of grotesque, linen-wrapped monstrosities shambling through ancient ruins. However, echoes of removing moisture of the cadaver can be seen in modern funeral parlours where embalming the body is still practiced.

Ta-Kush is accompanied at the museum by a more-deathly artefact of cartonnage. Thought to be a mummified hawk for many years, a recent CT scan revealed the occupant of the sarcophagus to be a miscarried 20-week-old foetus. The gestational baby is one of the youngest human mummies in the world. Keeping human remains in museums for the sake of heritage poses moral dilemmas. Yet, through interpretive stories and multimedia technologies, the Maidstone Mummy teaches us many lessons.

Address Maidstone Museum, St Faith's Street, Maidstone, Kent, ME14 1LH, +44 (0)162 260 2838, www.museum.maidstone.gov.uk, museuminfo@maidstone.gov.uk | Getting there Train to Maidstone East or Maidstone Barracks | Hours See website for seasonal hours | Tip Visit the Coldrum Stones, a Neolithic burial site built 1000 years before Stonehenge (Coldrum Long Barrow, Coldrum Lane, Trottiscliffe, West Malling, Kent).

93__Old Operating Theatre

Imagined echoes of patients' pain

Within the garret (attic) of St Thomas' Church, at the site of the
original St Thomas' Hospital, is an atmospheric museum dedicated
to Georgian and Victorian surgical heritage. The museum displays
medical procedures and operations that pre-date anaesthetics and
antiseptics. As the hospital adjoined the church, it houses the oldest
surviving operating theatre in Europe.

Built in 1822, the garret had two operating theatres, one for men
and one for women. Only the women's theatre survives today. As
female patients were carried from nearby wards, banks of seats in
the theatre allowed medical students to watch proceedings. With
only opiates and alcohol to dull the pain, the faster the surgeon
performed his work, the greater the chance that the patient survived. Some surgeons performed amputations in less than a min-
ute (see ch. 110). Unsanitary conditions prevailed, with sawdust on
the floor to sop up blood and pus. The garret was also home to an
apothecary, where medicinal herbal remedies were stored. Opium
poppies were discovered in the timber rafters. Today, the garret,
like the theatre, has been reconstructed to convey an eerie sense of
pre-modern healthcare.

St Thomas' Hospital has always been a teaching institution. It
moved in 1862 to its present location in Lambert. A church has
existed on the site of St Thomas' since 1106 and was re-dedicated to
St Thomas the Apostle in 1540 after the Catholic martyr St Thomas
Becket had been de-canonised during the Reformation. St Thomas'
was rebuilt between 1698 and 1702 by Christopher Wren's chief
mason, Thomas Cartwright. In 1859, Florence Nightingale, the
founder of modern nursing, set up her nursing school at St Thomas'.
The operating theatre was forgotten until it was rediscovered in
1956 by historian Raymond Russell and opened as a museum in
1962. Visitors are greeted by the imagined echoes of patients' pain.

Address 9a St Thomas Street, London, SE1 9RY, +44 (0)207 188 2679, www.oldoperatingtheatre.com | Getting there Tube to London Bridge (Jubilee and Northern Lines) | Hours Fri & Sat 10:30am–5pm | Tip There's a charming monument dedicated to Hodge the Cat, Dr Samuel Johnson's favourite feline (17 Gough Square, London, www.talkingstatueslondon.co.uk/statues/hodge).

94 Postman's Park
Memorial to heroic self-sacrifice

Postman's Park is a little-known memorial to ordinary people killed in tragic misfortunes. In a tranquil garden, not far from St Paul's Cathedral, this monument commemorates ordinary people in extraordinary situations. Described as 'The People's Westminster Abbey', visitors can observe a poignant reminder of past unassuming heroes. People who died in workplace accidents or perished saving others and who might have faded into history are remembered.

First proposed in 1887 by George Frederic Watts to commemorate the Golden Jubilee of Queen Victoria, the memorial pays homage to humble heroes. With 62 acts of self-sacrifice between 1863 and 2009, the memorial was originally inspired by a passage in George Eliot's 1866 novel Felix Holt: 'A monument to the faithful who were not famous, and who are precious as the continuity of the sunbeams is precious, though some of them fall unseen and on barrenness.'

Despite this inspiration, George Watts's idea for a memorial met with indifference from potential patrons. However, Watts wrote to *The Times* on 7 September, 1887, expounding his idea for 'Another Jubilee Suggestion'. He stated, 'It must surely be a matter of regret when names worthy to be remembered and stories stimulating and instructive are allowed to be forgotten. It is not too much to say that the history of Her Majesty's reign would gain a lustre were the nation to erect a monument, say, here in London, to record the names of these likely to be forgotten heroes.'

The monument to the heroes of humble life was completed in 1900. One of the first tablets commemorated the deeds of a labourer, who was fatally scalded at the Battersea Sugar Works trying to save his workmate. George Watts was too ill to attend the unveiling ceremony and died in 1904. Visitors today can see how society reacts to the ordinary heroic dead with posthumous recognition.

Address Postman's Park, St Martin's Le Grand, London, EC1A 7BT, www.postmanspark.org.uk | Getting there Tube to St Paul's (Central Line) | Hours Daily 8am–dusk | Tip Pay a visit to the National Firefighters Memorial, a bronze monument depicting three firefighters battling flames during the Blitz of World War II (Carter Lane Gardens/Peter's Hill, Old Street, London).

95__ The Skateboard Graveyard
A skateboarding shrine for Timothy Baxter

A curious, informal memorial sits on the concrete platform that supports the Golden Jubilee Bridges across the River Thames between the Embankment and South Bank. Broken skateboards have been laid to rest, or perhaps *thrown* to rest, onto the bridge's substructure. The 'skateboard graveyard' is a community-based commemoration of a brutal murder and heinous attack on two young men on the evening of 18 June, 1999.

The Golden Jubilee Bridges honour Queen Elisabeth II's 50 years on the throne. Opened in 2002, the Golden Jubilee Bridges replaced a narrow, badly-lit footbridge where the murder occurred. The new bridges are partially attached to the Hungerford Bridge, which was originally erected by Isambard Kingdom Brunel in 1845. Close to the bridge is Southbank Skate Park, situated within an under-croft of the Southbank Centre. The park has been a spiritual den to London's skating community since the 1970s. It was from here that Timothy Baxter and his childhood friend Gabriel Cornish, both 24 and keen skateboarders, began to cross the bridge. Neither made it to the other side.

While on the bridge, they were accosted by three muggers. As the altercation grew, three more individuals arrived and joined the unprovoked attack. The mostly juvenile gang beat Timothy and Gabriel unconscious and dumped them into the river. Gabriel survived, but Timothy was lost. His body was found downstream the following day. The culprits, all from socially deprived and chaotic backgrounds, later received significant prison sentences.

As a tribute, skateboarders leave old boards on the bridge as an organic memorial to Timothy. Local authorities inadvertently 'cleaned up' the site in 2013, but more skateboards soon appeared. The act of a gratuitous violent attack is remembered through this skateboard shrine, where Timothy Baxter met his sad and senseless end.

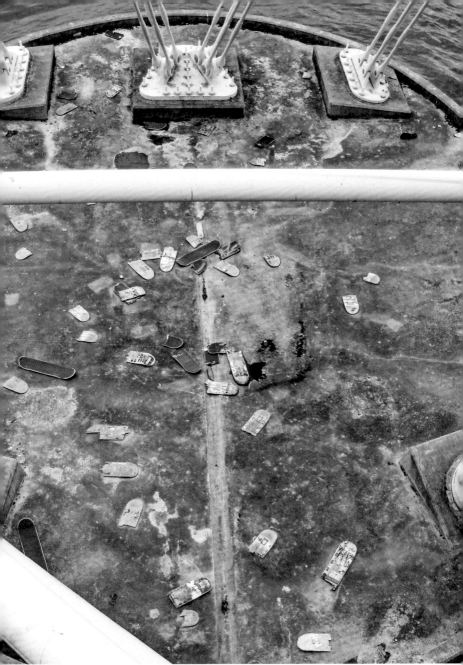

Address 9152 Golden Jubilee Bridges, Charing Cross, London, WC2N 6NS | Getting there Tube to Embankment (Bakerloo, Circle, District and Northern Lines) | Hours Unrestricted | Tip Visit the Charing Cross Storm Tree, a living memorial to all the trees lost during the Great Storm of 1987 near the entrance to Charing Cross Station in London.

96 Spencer Perceval Memorial

The only British PM to be assassinated

In the nave of Westminster Abbey is a memorial to former Prime Minister Spencer Perceval. Known as the 'evangelical prime minister', Perceval is the only British PM to have been assassinated. On 11 May, 1812, John Bellingham, a bankrupt man with grievances against the Government, shot Perceval in the lobby of the House of Commons.

Perceval was born in 1762 to the 2nd Earl of Egmont and educated at Harrow and Trinity College Cambridge. In 1790, he married Jane Wilson and had 12 children. As a lawyer, he became a Member of Parliament in 1796 and PM in 1809. Perceval was a small, slight and pale man who never sat for a full-sized portrait. A marble bust of Perceval based on his death mask by Joseph Nollekens is displayed at Pitzhanger Manor in Ealing. Perceval railed against the Catholic Emancipation, which reduced many restrictions made on Roman Catholics by the Penal Laws. He was also against parliamentary reform but did support the abolition of the slave trade. Perceval was seen as a devout and pious man who strongly objected to hunting, drinking and adultery. As prime minister, he oversaw the political crisis of the madness of King George III.

John Bellingham was a merchant broker born in 1769. His work took him to Russia, and in 1804, he had his travelling pass confiscated because of alleged debts. Bellingham was jailed in Russia and released in 1809. Once home, he petitioned the government for compensation for his imprisonment to no avail. Holding a grudge, Bellingham shot Perceval in the heart and then sat calmly on a bench. After claiming he wished he had assassinated the British Ambassador to Russia, he was hanged on 15 May, 1812. His skull is housed at Barts Pathology Museum (see ch. 78). A memorial to Perceval was unveiled in 1822 with sculptured allegorical figures representing Power, Truth and Temperance overlooking the dead prime minister.

Address Westminster Abbey, 20 Dean Yard, Westminster, London, SW1 3PA, www.westminster-abbey.org | Getting there Tube to Westminster (Circle, District and Jubilee Lines) | Hours See website for seasonal hours | Tip See the fully dressed, preserved auto-icon of Jeremy Bentham (1748 – 1832), founder of modern utilitarianism, at the University College London Student Centre (Student 27 – 28 Gordon Square, London, www.ucl.ac.uk/culture/auto-icon).

97 St Bride's Charnel House

A hidden world of the dead revealed in the Blitz

St Bride's Church is woven into the historical fabric of London. Resting on a site that has seen at least eight reincarnations of a church dating back almost 2,000 years and famed for its tiered spire that is plagiarised by wedding cake bakers the world over, St Bride's holds a secret. It is built on seven crypts, two medieval charnel houses and over 7,000 bodies. The skeletal remains are meters deep and yet to be fully excavated.

St Bride's is known as the 'Journalist's Church' for its location within the former journalistic hub of Fleet Street and the first modern printing press set up in 1500 by Wynkyn de Worde. Irish missionaries built the church atop Roman foundations in the 6th century and named it after St Bride, the daughter of an Irish prince. A succession of buildings followed until St Bride's was destroyed in the Great Fire of London in 1666. Under the inspired direction of Christopher Wren (see ch. 98), the church was rebuilt and was his second most expensive church after St Paul's Cathedral.

During the Blitz of World War II in 1940, German incendiary bombs reduced Wren's architectural gem to a shell. In 1953, the church was rebuilt to Wren's original design, and during the reconstruction, archaeologist W.F. Grimes discovered the hidden burial chambers that lay beneath.

Many of the dead were Great Plague victims from 1665 while others had succumbed to the 1854 cholera epidemic in London when Parliament ordered all crypts to be sealed. The crypt contains an iron coffin to ward off Victorian-era body snatchers as the trade in anatomical cadavers was big business at that time (see ch. 110). Corpses of children were sold by the inch and adults by their body parts. Having survived the corpse trade and the Blitz, St Bride's is home to an important scientific resource of skeletal remains. Today, visitors can explore this underground world of the dead.

Address St Bride's Church, Fleet Street, London, EC4Y 8AU, +44 (0)207 427 0133, www.stbrides.com, stb@stbrides.com | Getting there Tube to Blackfriars (Circle and District Lines) | Hours Mon–Fri 8am–5pm, Sat 10am–3.30pm, Sun 9.30am–4pm | Tip Visit Holy Sepulchre Church to see the Execution Bell, which rang 12 times on the eve of a convict's hanging (Holborn Viaduct, Farringdon, London).

98__ St Dunstan-in-the-East

A bombed out church and urban oasis

Within the hectic metropolis of the City of London lies a green oasis born out of bombs and suffering. St Dunstan-in-the-East was an Anglian church halfway between London Bridge and the Tower of London. The church is named after Dunstan, a former Dark Ages statesman and Archbishop of Canterbury famed for pulling the Devil's nose with red-hot tongs. The church was originally built around 1100, and a new aisle was added in 1391 and repaired again in 1631. However, the Great Fire of London in 1666 (see ch. 29) saw the church partially destroyed. Christopher Wren (see ch. 97) added a new gothic style spire in 1695. Due to inherent structural problems, the church was rebuilt by David Laing in 1817.

The church remained until 1941, when the Nazis launched the Blitz bombing campaign against London. As World War II transformed into a war on society and industry, German bombers dropped tons of high explosives and thousands of incendiary bombs on the city. Over 43,500 civilians were killed and many more injured or made homeless. During the bombing siege, St Dunstan Church was hit and largely destroyed. Only Wren's tower and the north and south walls survived. After the war and following a reorganisation of the Anglian dioceses, it was decided not to rebuild the church. In 1967, the City of London Corporation turned the ruins into a public garden, with horticultural planting and a small fountain in the middle of the nave. The ruins and gardens opened to the public in 1971.

The ruins of St Dunstan are a tranquil *heterotopia* – a space that has been arrested in time. It is a serene place of juxtapositions, where the familiar and uncanny collide. Sprawling greenery emerges from the devastation of war, creating an enchanting urban sanctuary. City slickers mix with tourists in this refuge from modernity. The war dead are long passed, but Mother Nature has turned carnage into catharsis.

Address St Dunstan's Hill, Billingsgate, London, EC3R 5DD, +44 (0)207 374 4127, www.cityoflondon.gov.uk | Getting there Tube to Monument (Circle and District Lines) | Hours Daily 8am–dusk | Tip Look for the 202-foot-tall memorial to the Great Fire of London designed by Wren and built with a secret underground laboratory on Monument Street (15 Monument Street, London, www.themonument.org.uk).

99 __ St Leonard's Ossuary

Coming face to face with our dead

Built around 1090, St Leonard's Church in the coastal market town of Hythe is home to the best-preserved collection of medieval human skulls and bones in Britain. St Leonard is the Patron Saint of Prisoners; yet in the church's ossuary (crypt) are the remains of over 4,000 people. Reassembled into collections in 1910, the ossuary has more women than men and nearly 10 per cent of the bones are from children.

The bones are likely to be from area residents in the 13th century and were dug from graves when extra burial grounds were required. Other theories of origin include the bones of Danish pirates slain in battle, men who fell in the 1066 Battle of Hastings or victims of the Black Death (although such bodies were usually disposed of in quicklime). The earliest references to the 'church with the bones' are from 1678 by the Town Clerk of Rye, Samuel Jeake, and from 1679 by the Chaplain to the Cinque Ports Rev Brome. They both describe 'an orderly pile of dead men's bones' in the 'charnel house'. Early drawings of the ossuary date from 1787, and postcards in the 1900s suggest the bones were a tourist attraction in Edwardian England. The church has long charged a fee to see the bones. After the 1170 assassination of St Thomas Becket, the Archbishop of Canterbury charged people who searched for his relics. The practice of storing fleshed bones in ossuaries was commonplace during the medieval period but died out in England after the Reformation.

Evidence of ill health and vitamin deficiency can be seen in the bones. Skulls with fractures suggest a brutal end for some of the deceased. In the 1960s, a skull was stolen and eventually returned by a man who pretended it was a murder victim. In 2018, 21 skulls were stolen, and they may have been sold on the black market. The bones mediate a sense of mortality as we come face to face with our ancestral dead.

Address St Leonard's Church, Oak Walk, Hythe, Kent, CT21 5DN, +44 (0)130 326 2370, www.slhk.org/theossuary.htm | Getting there Train to Sandling | Hours See website for seasonal and holiday hours | Tip Saltwood Castle is the scene of assassination plots against Thomas Becket, 'heretic' persecution, and Nazi conspiracies (Hythe, Kent, CT21 4QU, www.saltwoodcastle.com).

100__ Stairway to Heaven
Crushed to death fleeing a false air raid warning

On 3 March, 1943, one of the worst civilian disasters of World War II struck Bethnal Green tube station. The London Underground transit system stations were often used as civilian bomb shelters to protect Londoners from Nazi bombs. On that fateful night, locals headed for Bethnal Green station after hearing an air raid warning. At 8.27pm, three double decker buses arrived, carrying more people from pubs, clubs and cinemas. At the same time, a new anti-aircraft rocket was fired, causing a sound unfamiliar to locals. Thinking it was a German weapon, people panicked and ran into the single entrance to the station.

Unbeknown to the crowd trying to get in, a woman carrying a baby had slipped on the lower steps, causing her to topple another man. As they tried to clamber to their feet, the surge of a panic-stricken crowd behind them in the stairway meant more people stumbled and fell. Over 300 people became trapped in a chaotic melee and jammed solid between the bottom of the stairs and the ceiling. Pinned down by the weight of so many bodies, 173 people were killed through asphyxiation and crushing, including 62 children and babies. Entire generations of families were wiped out in the disaster. By 11.40pm, corpses were laid outside a nearby pub, with organs spilling through mouths as compression injuries became apparent. With bitter irony, no enemy air raids were reported over Bethnal Green that night.

The government, fearing for wartime morale, did not acknowledge pre-warned health and safety issues of the stairway but chose to blame a German bomb for the incident. In 2017, after years of activism and fundraising, including by local resident Harry Paticas, the Stairway to Heaven Memorial was unveiled. The solid teak sculpture with conical shaped holes inverts a negative space, creating a place to reflect on the tragedy and honour those who died.

Address Bethnal Green Gardens, Bethnal Green, London, E2 9QX, +44 (0)207 364 5000 | Getting there Tube to Bethnal Green (Central Line) | Hours Unrestricted | Tip See the Blue Plaque marking the first V1 Flying Bomb (or Doodlebug) to fall on London in 1944 (Grove Road, Railway Bridge, Bow, London).

101__Ten Bells Public House

'From Hell' to the abyss

The Ten Bells pub located in Spitalfields has existed in one guise or another since the mid-1750s. A tiled mural in the pub pays homage to bygone Spitalfields and its weaving heritage. The pub also has connections with the Kray Twins gangsters in the 1960s (see ch. 111). In 1888, the pub was catapulted into murder folklore as the alleged place where two of Jack the Ripper's victims were last seen (see ch. 88).

The pub's name refers to the number of bells at the nearby Nicholas Hawksmoor-designed Christ Church. In 1755, the pub was known as the Eight Bells Alehouse but changed to Ten Bells when the church upgraded its bell tower. During the 18th century, the urban poor amassed in London's East End, including in Spitalfields and neighbouring Whitechapel. These were places of slums and extreme poverty. American novelist Jack London in 1902 described its residents as 'people of the Abyss'. The hellish connotation of the poor living in the depths was the backdrop for the Ripper serial murders of 1888. Within this 'abyss' was the Ten Bells pub, a raucous drinking den for the Victorian working classes. Annie Chapman is said to have been drinking at the pub before she became the second victim of Jack the Ripper. Mary Kelly is also said to have frequented the pub before she was mutilated as the final Ripper victim.

In 1976, the pub crassly changed its name to capitalise on its Ripper connections and was called Jack the Ripper. After a campaign by Reclaim the Night, the pub reverted to its original name in 1988. It is mentioned in the 1999 graphic novel *From Hell*, while the 2001 film adaptation shows Johnny Depp as Inspector Abberline having a drink with Mary Kelly in the pub. The great-great-grandfather of British celebrity chef Jamie Oliver was landlord of the Ten Bell in the 1880s, and he may have met Annie Chapman and Mary Kelly – or even Jack the Ripper!

Address 84 Commercial Street, Spitalfields, London, E1 6LY, +44 (0)207 247 7532, www.tenbells.com | Getting there Tube to Aldgate East (District and Hammersmith & City Lines) or Liverpool Street (Central, Circle and Hammersmith & City Lines) | Hours Sun–Wed noon–midnight, Thu–Sat noon–1am | Tip Arnold Circus is a celebrated bandstand at the centre of what was once London's worst slum (Boundary Gardens, Shoreditch).

102 Tower of London Terrors

A prison and place of persecution

Sitting strategically on the River Thames is one of England's most iconic structures. The Tower of London, a castle constructed by William the Conqueror in 1066, reflected a resented symbol of oppression of Norman-French subjugation. The tower now represents the last military conquest of England. To control the Tower of London was to control the country.

The White Tower at the heart of the castle buildings was built in 1078. It was developed during the 12th and 13th centuries to sit within two concentric rings of defensive walls and a moat. The tower has served in different capacities through its illustrious history as an armoury, a treasury and the Royal Mint, a menagerie, a public record office, and home to the Crown Jewels of England. The tower has also been a royal residence. Yet, it is best known as a prison and place of persecution.

Anne Boleyn was executed at the tower in 1536 at the bequest of her husband, Henry VIII. Guy Fawkes was tortured and executed for the 1605 Gunpowder Plot. During World War I, 11 men were executed by firing squad for espionage. And in 1941, Rudolf Hess, Adolf Hitler's deputy, was the last state prisoner, as he tried to broker a peace deal. The last person to be executed at the tower was German spy Josef Jakobs, who was shot on 15 August, 1941.

However, the macabre reputation of the Tower has been exaggerated, particularly by the 16th-century religious propagandists and 19th-century romanticists. Whilst the Tower has been a visitor attraction since the Elizabethan period, the writings of William Harrison Ainsworth have been influential. His 1840 novel, *The Tower of London: A Historical Romance*, created vivid descriptions of torture chambers and devices to brutalise prisoners. Tales of torment and horrific abuse to extract confessions are the images that stuck in the public imagination, including visitors today.

Address Tower Hamlets, London, EC3N 4AB, www.hrp.org.uk/tower-of-london | **Getting there** Tube to Tower Hill (Circle and District Lines) or London Bridge (Jubilee and Northern Lines) | **Hours** See website for hours | **Tip** Visit the 'Ghost Stations' of the London Underground transit system, which are abandoned Tube stations that exist beneath the streets. Guided tours only (www.ltmuseum.co.uk/hidden-london).

103 Wildgoose Memorial Library

A mysterious memento mori

Somewhere in Central London is a depository of curiosities that narrates our sense of mortality. The Wildgoose Memorial Library (WML) is the idea of Dr Jane Wildgoose, an artist and curator whose collections focus on death and dying. As keeper of her own private academy, Wildgoose presides over a 'memory theatre' of provocative artefacts. The WML includes many skulls, statuettes, medical pots, taxidermy pieces and even a replica of Lord Nelson's coffin. As Wildgoose states, her objects are 'designed to facilitate meditation and free associations on subjects pertaining to the mysteries of the living in relation to the dead, transience, memory and immortality.' The WML mystifies further by having no registered address and welcoming interested visitors by appointment only. It is an oasis of curios on universal themes of life and death.

The WML began life with Wildgoose's artistic fascination with the dead and their fundamental interrelationships with the living. The ongoing accumulation of reference material took on a formal stance in 2003, when the WML was featured in the BBC Radio 4 documentary *On One Lost Hair*. It follows Wildgoose and others purchasing a piece of hair of Lord Horatio Nelson, saviour of the British Empire and hero of Trafalgar. The hair was sold as an item on eBay, and the programme follows its final journey as it is liberated into the River Thames. Wildgoose exposes the different strands of the story, including the absurdities on commoditization of death materials, ethics and ownership, and authenticity of relics.

Wildgoose is currently investigating the potential for a more public-facing home for the WML. Part artist studio, part reliquary, part research centre, the WML is a fascinating *memento mori*, where objects mediate a symbolic reminder of the inevitability of death.

Address By request only, www.janewildgoose.co.uk, wildgoose@janewildgoose.co.uk | Hours
Email Dr Jane Wildgoose for an appointment | Tip Visit the Sir John Franklin Expedition
Memorial, a tribute to the ill-fated search for the Northwest Passage aboard HMS *Erebus*
and HMS *Terror* in 1845 at the Old Royal Naval College (Chapel of St Peter & St Paul,
Greenwich, London, www.ornc.org).

104 Women of WWII Memorial

Remembering all women who served

"Let the women of Britain come forward!" proclaimed Winston Churchill. During World War II, over seven million women rallied to his call and served in the military and in munitions factories, agriculture and the Land Army. By 1943, nine out of 10 single women between the ages of 20 and 30 were serving. Over 450,000 women were conscripted into the armed forces. While men faced bloody battlefields, women made a huge yet often overlooked contribution to the war effort.

However, it was not until 9 July, 2005 that a national memorial to honour their contributions was created. The Memorial to the Women of World War II, designed by John W. Mills, was unveiled by Queen Elizabeth II and dedicated by Baroness Boothroyd, the former Speaker of the House of Commons. Part of the memorial funding was raised by Boothroyd during a celebrity edition of TV's *Who Wants to Be a Millionaire* in 2002.

Located on Whitehall, the bronze monument, 6.7 metres high by 1.8 metres wide, is a companion, or even competitor to the nearby Cenotaph. The 'Glorious Dead' that the Cenotaph commemorates might be assumed to relate to exclusively men, while the memorial to women replaces a statue of Sir Walter Raleigh that was moved to Greenwich. Gender issues and 'monument wars' aside, the memorial depicts 17 sets of clothing and uniforms around its sides, symbolising hundreds of jobs that women undertook – and largely relinquished back to men following the war. Outfits include a Red Cross nursing cape, a police overall, a welding mask and uniforms from the Land Army, Air Wardens and Women's Royal Navy Service. As a tribute to an entire generation of women, Baroness Boothroyd said in her dedication, 'It depicts the women's working clothes and how they quietly took them off at the end of the day, hung them up and let the men take the credit.'

THE WOMEN OF WORLD WAR II

Address Whitehall, London, SW1A 2NP, www.iwm.org.uk/memorials/item/memorial/
51288 | Getting there Tube to Westminster (Circle, District and Jubilee Lines) | Hours
Unrestricted | Tip Visit the Churchill War Rooms and discover a secret underground
labyrinth that housed the British Government during World War II (Clive Steps, King
Charles Street, London, www.iwm.org.uk/visits/churchill-war-rooms).

105 25 Cromwell Street

Memorial absence at the 'House of Horrors'

Fred and Rosemary West were husband-and-wife serial killers who murdered at least 12 young women between 1967 and 1987. The murders involved the Wests' warped sexual gratification, including incest and torture. Victims included Heather West – their 16-year-old daughter – who was buried in the garden at 25 Cromwell Street. Fred West even got his unwitting son to dig a hole for Heather's grave by lying about it being a fishpond, and he later paved it over as a patio. Victims were mutilated and buried in the cellar or garden at the address – a place that the media termed 'House of Horrors'. Fred West also murdered his 8-year-old daughter Charmaine and buried her at his house in nearby Midland Road.

One of the victims, 19-year-old Lynda Gough, was found under the cellar floor, dismembered and decapitated with many of her bones missing. Her jaw was wrapped in surgical tape to silence her screams, with two small plastic tubes inserted into her nasal cavities to allow breathing. Lynda had likely been suspended from the cellar ceiling, sexually abused by Fred and Rosemary, and then killed by strangulation. Fred later concreted the cellar floor and made it into a bedroom for his children. Arrested in 1994, Fred West escaped justice by committing suicide at Birmingham Prison before his trial. Rose West was convicted of 10 murders and is now serving a life prison sentence.

In 1996, Gloucestershire County Council decided to demolish the house at 25 Cromwell Street for fear of macabre souvenir hunters. An unassuming walkway is all that is left of the murder house, with no memorial to the victims. While the physical evidence is now obliterated, the absence of commemoration leaves a contradictory space. The inconspicuous pathway on which this building once stood is where visitors should remember the victims, as their plight should never be forgotten.

Address 25 Cromwell Street, Gloucester, GL1 1RE | Getting there Train to Gloucester, then a 15-minute walk | Hours Unrestricted from the outside only | Tip Purton Hulks is the largest ship graveyard in mainland Britain and well worth a visit to see the abandoned vessels (Berkeley, Gloucestershire).

106 Anti-Slavery Arch

Reminder of a shameful past and a call to action

With the support of HM Queen Elizabeth I in 1573, the British nefarious trade – enslavement of people – lasted until its abolition in 1807 (see ch. 46). Great Britain was the premier slave trader, sending African men, women and children to European colonies in the Americas by force in exchange for manufactured goods or raw materials. Millions of people were transported during the period, and many hundreds of thousands died as a result of their horrendous journey and ill-treatment. Nearby Bristol prospered on the back of slavery and grew rich as a port that traded humans.

The imposing stone arch in Stroud stands as a reminder of our shameful past, as well as a celebration of progress. The *Abolition of Slavery Act 1833* ended slavery across the British Empire. To commemorate the event, Henry Wyatt (1793–1847), a wealthy local philanthropist and member of the Stroud Anti-Slavery Society, erected the Anti-Slavery Arch in 1834. It originally formed the entrance to a grand Georgian mansion and Wyatt's Farmhill Park estate. The Arch is the UK's oldest monument to the abolition of slavery.

Restored in 1960-61 and again in 2001, the Historic England Grade II Listed monument marks the positive cultural shift that ended slavery and spelled freedom for up to a million people. The Arch is a marker in our landscape where we can stop and pay respects to those denied freedom, and to those abolitionists who worked to make slavery illegal.

However, it is disturbing to reflect that slavery across the world is still a problem today. The UN International Labour Organisation estimates that about 25 million people, including many in the UK, are victims of modern-day slavery. Many are forced to work in textile or construction industries, or in domestic service. The commemorative plaque adjacent to the Arch reads: *"The fight to end modern day slavery continues world wide"*.

Address Memorial Arch, Stroud, Goucestershire, GL5 4BT, www.stroudpreservationtrust.org.uk/the-anti-slavery-arch.html, sptrust30@gmail.com | Getting there Train to Stroud, then walk to the junction of Farm Hill Land and Paganhill Estate | Hours Unrestricted | Tip Crawl inside a 5,000-year-old Neolithic tomb at Uley Long Barrow (Coaley, Dursley, www.english-heritage.org.uk/visit/places/uley-long-barrow-hetty-peglers-tump).

107 __ Bodmin Gaol

Home of 'Long Drop' hanging

Built in 1779 using French prisoners of war, Bodmin Gaol (jail) was the site of 55 public executions until its closure in 1927. Mainly used as a debtor prison and later as a naval jail for the British Admiralty, Bodmin Gaol lies nestled in the civil parish of Bodmin in Cornwall, on the outskirts of mythical Bodmin Moor. It hosts the only 'working' execution pit in the UK, discovered during renovation works in 2005. The pit highlights how the condemned were dispatched with 'long drop' hanging.

William Marwood, a hangman at Bodmin Gaol (1872–1883), was a pioneer of the 'long drop'. With his method of hanging, each culprit received a drop of eight feet, making death instantaneous. Before this method, prisoners were often left dangling at the end of a shorter rope and died by strangulation, often in front of a spectator crowd. Marwood was so successful as a hangman that he said, 'I prefer to be called an executioner'. Local children even composed a rhyme about his slayer deeds: *If Pa killed Ma, who'd kill Pa? – Marwood.*

Viewed as one of Britain's most haunted buildings, the jail hosts 'After Dark' paranormal tours – with dinner included! The ghost of Selina Wadge, hanged in 1900 for the murder of her son, Harry, is reported to appear as a full-torso manifestation. She had thrown Harry into a 13-foot well, where the young lad drowned. Apparently, her apparition tries to reach out to small children and to instill guilt and remorse on pregnant women. The last person hanged was in 1909, and the jail closed in 1927. Presently, there are no prisons within the county of Cornwall.

Steeped in social and architectural history, the former gaol has undergone a £30 million redevelopment to turn it into quite an unusual 63-bed hotel and visitor attraction. But Bodmin Gaol will continue to offer visitors an intriguing insight into often-brutal penal life over the centuries.

Address Berrycoombe Road, Bodmin, Cornwall, PL31 2NR, +44 (0)120 876 292, www.bodminjail.org, info@bodminjail.org | Getting there Train to Bodmin General, then walk 15 minutes | Hours Daily 9.30am – 8.30pm | Tip Daphne du Maurier's *Jamaica Inn* is a tale of smugglers and murderers in Bolventor, and the actual inn welcomes visitors for drinks, dinner or a weekend stay (Bolventor Bodmin Moor, Cornwall, www.jamaicainn.co.uk).

108__ Broadway Tower
A folly and a Cold War bunker

Broadway Tower is a folly on Broadway Hill, near the picturesque village of Broadway. Overlooking the Vale of Evesham towards the Malvern Hills, and at 312 metres above sea level, it is the second highest point in the Cotswolds (after Cleeve Hill). The 'Saxon' tower stands at 20 metres tall and was designed by Lancelot 'Capability' Brown and James Wyatt in 1794. It was built for Lady Coventry in 1798, who wondered if she could see a lit beacon from her home in Worcester, 22 miles away. Indeed, the tower and beacon could be seen clearly.

The tower housed a printing press in the early 1800s, owned by book collector Sir Thomas Phillipps. It was later reserved as a Romantic artist retreat for pre-Raphaelite painters, including William Morris, Dante Gabriel Rossetti and Edward Burne-Jones. However, in the late 1950s, Broadway was chosen to monitor deadly radioactive fallout in the event of a nuclear war.

The Royal Observer Corps underground bunker was built 46 meters from the tower and manned continuously from 1961 until it was decommissioned in 1991. The former monitoring bunker was once part of a network of similar structures across the UK to detect incoming nuclear missiles and report effects of atomic explosions. The bunker was one of the last Cold War bunkers to be constructed and is now one of a few fully equipped facilities left in England. Restored extensively in 2011, this small bunker is open for visitors to discover what life was like for Cold War volunteers. The only way in is down a ladder, so visitors should be prepared to climb.

Broadway Tower and Country Park is located on the Cotswold Way, with various exhibitions, as well as a gift shop and restaurant. A war memorial adjacent to the tower commemorates five aircrew of an AW38 Whitley bomber that crashed less than 200 yards from the tower during a training mission in June 1943.

Address Broadway Tower, Middle Hill, Broadway, Worcestershire, WR12 7LB, +44 (0)138 685 2945, www.broadwaytower.co.uk, office@broadwaytower.co.uk | **Getting there** Train to Evesham, then a 15-minute taxi ride | **Hours** Daily 10am–5pm | **Tip** The tree-framed door at St Edward's Church possibly inspired J.R.R. Tolkien's 'Doors of Durin' (2 Crossways House, The Square, Stow-on-the-Wold).

109___ Cheddar Gorge & Caves

Our ancestors ate their dead

In 1892, Captain Richard Cox Gough excavated what is now Gough's Cave, a 155-metre deep and 3.4km-long cavern, located within Cheddar Gorge in the Mendip Hills. Containing the Cheddar Yeo, the largest underground river system in Britain, the caves also held skeletal human remains from 14,700 years ago. All the remains showed cut-marks and butchered breakages consistent with cannibalism.

Skull fragments are from up to seven humans, including a three-year-old child and two adolescents. The skulls and brain cases were prepared as drinking cups – a ritualistic tradition discovered in other Magdalenian sites across Europe. In what is now spectacular scenery of rural Somerset, our ancestors were ritualistically eating their dead at the end of the Ice Age.

Cannibalism may have been a way of disposing of the dead – different in practice, but not in meaning to cremations or burials. There are no signs that individuals suffered violent deaths before being eaten. Engraving found on bones may have been a form of remembrance, and animal bones also discovered in the cave suggest that the practice of cannibalism was a cultural choice, not due to hunger. In 1903, Britain's oldest and most complete human skeleton was discovered further inside Gough's Cave. Nicknamed 'Cheddar Man', the Mesolithic hunter-gatherer died approximately 7150 BC. His remains now reside at the Natural History Museum in London with a replica at the Cannibals Museum.

The museum is not for the faint-hearted. It demonstrates our ancient past, where consuming another individual was a way of life. Cannibalism is a common ecological interaction in the animal kingdom, as it regulates populations and offers additional food sources. The lives and deaths of our ancestors were often brutal. They were indeed cannibals, and the museum attempts to provide context as to how and why they were.

Address Cheddar, Somerset, BS27 3QF, www.cheddargorge.co.uk, info@cheddargorge.co.uk | Getting there Train to Weston-Super-Mare, then transfer to bus 126 to Wells | Hours See website | Tip Visit the unusual grave of Dion Fortune, one of the most important mystics and occultists of the 20th century (Wells Road, Glastonbury, BA6 9AG).

110 George Marshall Medical Museum

Macabre death masks and pseudoscience

George Marshall Medical Museum is home to a fascinating, if not macabre, collection of artefacts that illustrate how healthcare has evolved over the past 300 years. George Marshall was born in Edinburgh in 1906 and practiced medicine from 1928. He became Consultant Surgeon at Worcester Royal Infirmary until his retirement in 1971. He once joked that he knew the people of Worcester "inside and out". Marshall was also an avid collector of old medical curios and surgical heritage, and he bequeathed his collection to the museum in the 1970s.

Located at the former infirmary, the museum has a reconstructed apothecary's shop and a 19th-century operating theatre. The infirmary opened in 1746, about 100 years before the advent of anaesthetics – the gory amputation chair is on display. Rare medical books, photographic archives, oral histories, bygone medical equipment and surgical displays make up the rest of the collection.

Gruesome death masks are believed to bear the faces of executed criminals from the early 19th century. Corpses of prisoners hanged in nearby Worcester Gaol were transported through an underground tunnel directly to the infirmary. Dissected by anatomists, the cadavers were an important aspect of medical education at the time (see ch. 85). However, making death masks of criminals was common, partly due to the pseudoscience of phrenology, or the measurement of bumps on the skull to predict mental traits. Convicts' death masks were used to attempt to connect physical features with crimes committed in order to predict future criminal behaviour. Finally discredited, phrenology had sinister connotations among those who argued for white supremacy. The nameless masks now provide a haunting glimpse of a dark episode of early medical science.

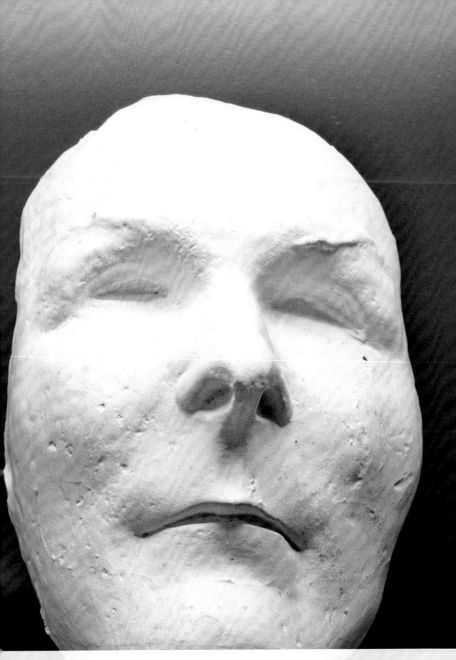

Address Worcestershire Royal Hospital, Charles Hastings Way, Worcester, WR5 1DD, +44 (0)190 576 3333, www.medicalmuseum.org.uk | Getting there Train to Worcester Shrub Hill, then a brief taxi ride | Hours Mon–Fri 9am–5pm | Tip Enjoy an interactive exhibition at the University of Worcester, where you'll explore one of England's oldest infirmaries (City Campus, Castle Street, Worcester).

111 Littledean Jail
'Alcatraz of the Forest'

Standing at the gateway of the Royal Forest of Dean is a former prison steeped in history and infamy. Conceived by prison reformer Sir George Onesiphorus Paul and built by leading prison architect of the day William Blackburn, Littledean Jail was a revolutionary House of Correction. Built in 1791, it became a model for London's Pentonville Prison, as well as for the Philadelphian Cherry Hill Penitentiary System in the United States. The first prisoner was 19-year-old Joseph Marshall, who stole a spade. Children were also incarcerated and often whipped with a birch rod. Other inmates included murderers, petty criminals, and women accused of 'witchcraft'.

Littledean Jail closed in 1854 and became a police station and remand centre, and a sessional court from 1874. It was also used as a stable for the Gloucestershire mounted police and an archive store for Gloucester Cathedral during World War II.

In 2003, the building was acquired by avid crime collector Andy Jones, who currently lives at the prison. Jones opened his controversial 'Crime Through Time' collection and turned Littledean Jail into what has been dubbed the 'world's sickest museum'. Despite receiving death threats and publicly battling with local authorities, Jones has created a macabre assemblage of crime-related oddities and memorabilia for visitors to the jail.

The unorthodox and un-curated corpus of curiosities includes tools of serial killer Fred West (see ch. 105), clothes from murderer Myra Hindley, and the tracksuit of paedophile Jimmy Saville. Provenance issues aside, the attraction has exhibits on the criminal Kray Twins, the Ku Klux Klan and notorious prisoner Charles Bronson. Other items include Nazi uniforms, a model of a Holocaust execution, unused IRA grenades and even a lamp supposedly made of human skin. The attraction is akin to a postmodern freak show featuring villainous exploits.

Address Littledean Jail, Littledean, Gloucestershire, GL14 3NL, +44 (0)159 482 6659, www.littledeanjail.com | Getting there Train to Gloucester, then bus 22 Coleford to Primary School | Hours See website | Tip Visit the 'Temple of Vaccinia', where Dr Edward Jenner, the 'father of immunology', vaccinated people against deadly diseases – at Dr Jenner's House Museum (The Chantry, Church Lane, Berkeley, Gloucestershire, www.jennermuseum.com).

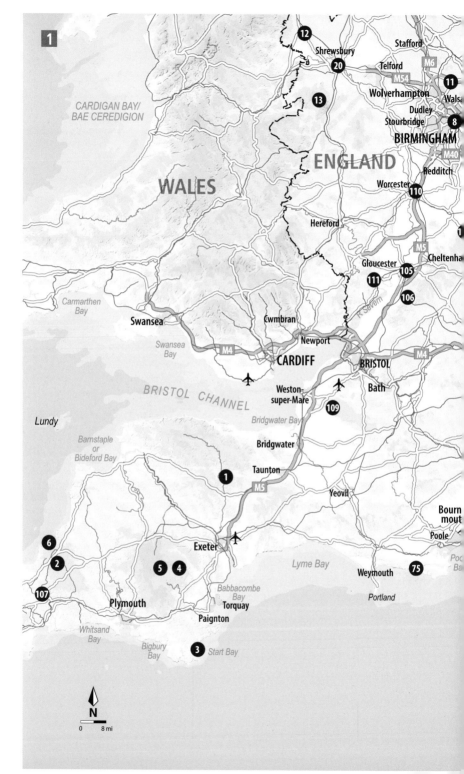

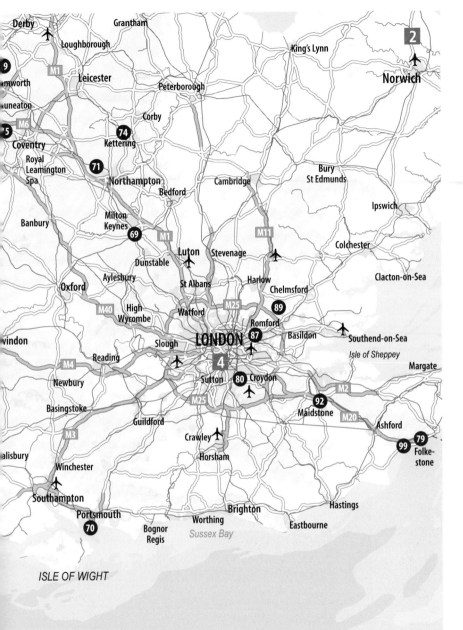

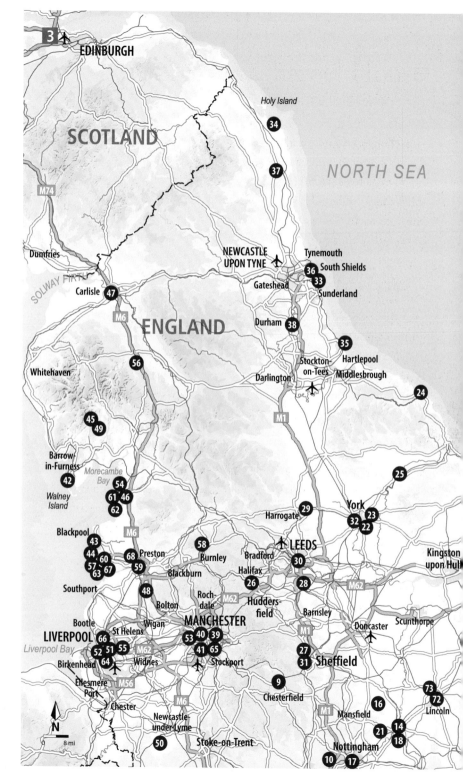

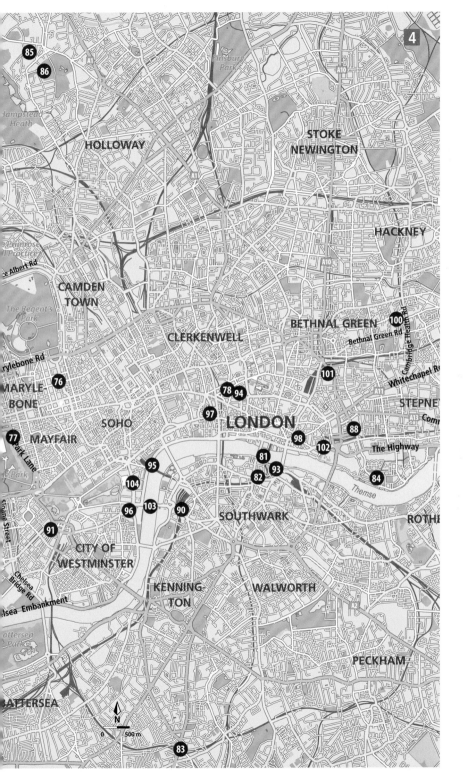

Photo credits

John Sykes, Birgit Weber
**111 Places in London
That You Shouldn't Miss**
ISBN 978-3-7408-1168-6

Ed Glinert, Marc Zakian
**111 Places in London's East
End That You Shouldn't Miss**
ISBN 978-3-7408-0752-8

Solange Berchemin,
Martin Dunford, Karin Tearle
**111 Places in Greenwich
That You Shouldn't Miss**
ISBN 978-3-7408-1107-5

Solange Berchemin
**111 Places in the Lake District
That You Shouldn't Miss**
ISBN 978-3-7408-0378-0

Rob Ganley, Ian Williams
**111 Places in Coventry
That You Shouldn't Miss**
ISBN 978-3-7408-1044-3

Martin Booth, Barbara Evripidou
**111 Places in Bristol
That You Shouldn't Miss**
ISBN 978-3-7408-0898-3

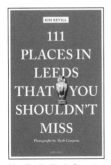

Kim Revill, Alesh Compton
**111 Places in Leeds
That You Shouldn't Miss**
ISBN 978-3-7408-0754-2

Julian Treuherz,
Peter de Figueiredo
**111 Places in Manchester
That You Shouldn't Miss**
ISBN 978-3-7408-0753-5

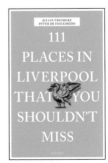

Julian Treuherz,
Peter de Figueiredo
**111 Places in Liverpool
That You Shouldn't Miss**
ISBN 978-3-95451-769-5

Acknowledgements

I would like to thank the following people for their valued insights and respected contributions in the making of this book: Aaron Stone, Sara Stone, David Stone, Stephen Stone, Katie Dorrian, Rachael Dorrian, Daniel Wright, Richard Sharpley, David Jarratt, Sean Gammon, Peter McGrath, and Stephen Moran... and everyone who stayed out of shot for my photos!

And, a special thank you to Karen Seiger and all her colleagues at Emons Verlag for inviting and helping me complete this poignant 'dark' project.

Gratiās vōbīs agō to one and all.

Philip R. Stone, Ph.D. is an internationally recognised scholar in the field of 'dark tourism' and 'difficult heritage'. He has published extensively about the subject in the academic literature and has presented his work at conferences across the world. Philip is also a media consultant on dark tourism, with clients including the BBC, CNN, *The New York Times*, *The Guardian*, and *The Washington Post*.